CONCEPT BOOKS · II

MORAL THINKING

CONCEPT BOOKS

General Editor: Alan Harris

MORAL THINKING

A guide for students

JOHN WILSON

Oxford University Department of Educational Studies

 HEINEMANN EDUCATIONAL BOOKS
LONDON

Heinemann Educational Books Ltd
LONDON EDINBURGH MELBOURNE AUCKLAND TORONTO
SINGAPORE HONG KONG KUALA LUMPUR
IBADAN NAIROBI JOHANNESBURG
NEW DELHI

ISBN 0 435 46190 7

Published in Great Britain by
Heinemann Educational Books Ltd
48 Charles Street, London W1X 8AH
Printed Offset Litho and bound by
Cox & Wyman Ltd
London, Fakenham and Reading

Contents

Preface

Morality is not something to be taken lightly. It is a form of thought and action, parallel to (though of course different from) other forms, such as science, history, the study of literature and so forth. Consequently it deserves study in its own right.

Schools and colleges have not, in general, given it what it deserves in this respect. This is not because teachers and educators have thought morality unimportant: but rather because most of them have had at best a confused picture, and at worst a false picture, of what moral thought and action is. The fault here has lain (if anywhere) not with the teachers and educators, but with the inability of most moral philosophers to communicate their findings effectively and intelligibly. Many schools and colleges have brought moral problems into their courses, often in an imaginative and stimulating way: and the interest of people in this area cannot be doubted. Our failure so far has been in how to satisfy this interest in a coherent way: briefly, in how to teach them what morality is about.

It would be naïve to suppose, of course, that the moral education of human beings depends chiefly on their mastering the concepts of morality here outlined. There are many other factors, of a psychological and sociological nature, which may well be more important, particularly for those whose capacity for thinking is limited. Some of these are outlined in our first publication (*Introduction to Moral Education*[1]), and I have drawn on this and other publications for some of the material in this book. But we ought not to underestimate the extent to which a direct approach of this kind may be effective. Anyone who is concerned with moral education ought, one would suppose, to try to explain

---

1 John Wilson *et al.*, Penguin Books, 1968: hereafter referred to as I.M.E.

what morality is and how to do it. At least this would help to remove the common impression that no such explanation is possible – that the whole thing is a complete muddle and not worth taking seriously. And it may not be too much to hope that conscious understanding of morality may make a good deal of practical difference to our lives.

I am grateful for the support of members of the Council and Steering Committee of the Farmington Trust: and in particular to Sir Nevill Mott, whose suggestion inspired the book in the first place.

J. B. W.

one

Thinking

What follows is supposed to help people think about what they ought to do, but it won't be of much use unless I start by making it plain why thinking is important and why it is difficult. By 'thinking' I don't mean just day-dreaming, or remembering, or wanting, or fearing, or having a feeling about something. I mean something more like using your brain, using words or other symbols to find an answer. Thinking is something which men do and most animals don't. Animals do all sorts of complicated things, but what they do is dictated to them by their instincts. They can't *think about* what they're doing, or make plans, or change their behaviour, or ask and answer questions. They just carry on doing whatever they do. But human beings have the power to forget what they're doing for the minute; they can take a mental step backwards, as it were, and consider whether what they're doing is right or wrong, sensible or stupid.

Just as human beings can stop doing things and think about doing them, so too they can stop saying things and think about what they're saying. They can wonder whether what they're saying is true or false, likely or unlikely, reasonable or unreasonable. This is what happens in arguments. If I say, 'The earth's flat' and you say, 'No, it's round', and we both just go on saying this over and over again, we can't get an argument started. The argument can only start when one of us stops saying, 'It's flat' or 'It's round', and begins to give *reasons* or offer *evidence*. Very young children who just say to each other, 'It is', 'It isn't', 'It is',

'It isn't', and go on saying so, aren't arguing and aren't thinking. It's only when they say things like, 'I think it is, *because* . . .' that they start thinking. But to say such things means putting their own views on one side for the time being, and very young children find this difficult.

As a matter of fact, all human beings find this difficult, not only children. Men have always disliked thinking, because it's hard work, and it seems easier not to bother. For many thousands of years men progressed at a snail's pace, doing exactly what their fathers had done, using primitive flint tools, living off what they could find in the way of roots and berries and the animals they could catch. Only very late in human history did they discover or invent things like the use of metals, agriculture, or reading and writing. Although these things are obviously useful, and don't really demand all that much intelligence to invent, they found it easier to go on doing what they had always done.

This is still true today. Although there are all sorts of highly developed arts and sciences, people still often think only when they have to. And people seem capable of putting up with an awful lot of difficulties before they feel that they must really start thinking about them and solving the necessary problems. We have very serious problems about war, and disease, and starvation, and insanity, and unhappiness, but we still don't spend much time thinking about them. We're prepared to complain about them, or to say how shocking they are, or we may even be willing to rush in and do something about them. But what we do may be mistaken, and we can't tell whether it is unless we think first.

The point of thinking, then, is simply that thinking is useful. It gets us what we want. It isn't just something which you are supposed to do at school because the teacher expects it, or because you have to pass exams, or because thinking is an 'educated' or 'cultural' thing to do. Quite a lot of people believe that they somehow ought to be 'intellectual' or 'cultural' – that it's more respectable or more upper-class if they pretend to enjoy reading books about history or philosophy. In the same way lots of people believe they ought to like classical music rather than pop music, because it makes them feel more cultured. But in fact if philosophy and other subjects which make you think are any good at all, they must have some point, or purpose, or use; just as, if classical music is more worth listening to than pop music, it must be because it has more to offer and gives more pleasure.

The difficulty with thinking (and perhaps with classical music too) is that it doesn't pay immediate dividends. You start by having a problem, and you have to resist the temptation to try and solve it too quickly. In order to solve it, you may need all sorts of techniques and ideas which don't, at first sight, seem to be connected with the problem in any obvious way. For instance, there are still some primitive peoples who build their bridges with immense labour out of plaited reeds and creepers. In order to teach them how to build proper bridges, which will bear a person's weight without collapsing, you have to teach them a bit of elementary mathematics. But this is very difficult: not because the mathematics itself is particularly hard, but because the primitive people don't see the point of it. They have to stop building their bridges the old way, and start learning things like the multiplication tables, which seem to them completely pointless and nothing to do with bridges at all.

Now this seems silly to us: but only because we know how mathematics is connected with bridge-building. There are plenty of techniques and ways of thinking which we often take to be pointless or silly, or a waste of time, or 'academic', or 'too abstract', but which are in fact essential for solving the problems we have. These are just those things that the primitive peoples say about mathematics; and indeed mathematics is, in a sense, an 'abstract' or 'academic' subject – only we couldn't get very far without it. Mathematics isn't as immediately exciting as flying aeroplanes, but without mathematics there wouldn't be any aeroplanes to fly.

B. ESCAPES FROM THINKING

Because thinking is hard work, we put up all sorts of resistances and defences against having to do it. Saying that it's 'too abstract' or 'academic' is only one of them. In this section we shall take a look at some of the ways in which people try to get out of the whole business of thinking. First some general points:

(a) It's true that people try to avoid thinking in quite ordinary, down-to-earth areas of living. For instance, a person may get fed up with trying to read the map, and say, 'Oh, well, let's not bother about which is the best way to go, let's just go this way'. Or someone who gets stomach-aches because he eats rich food that disagrees with him may not want to face up to the necessity of identifying and avoiding those foods. But, in these cases, people usually know well enough (if they're honest) that they're *not* thinking. They know, really, that they've evaded the issue. But when it comes to morals and politics and religion and problems about life in general, they don't usually admit it quite so easily. This is because there are all sorts of ways of *not* thinking, all sorts of ways of escaping thought, which are commonly regarded as *respectable*. Which ways these are depends on what society you live in. Thus in our society it wouldn't be thought by most people very respectable to consult an astrologer about how to live and whom to marry, or decide it by throwing dice, though it would have been in societies in the past. But phrases like 'what the Church says', 'what my friends do', 'what decent people feel', and 'what my conscience tells me' are all respectable alternatives to thinking. People can do 'what the Church says' or 'what my friends do' without losing face, or without seeming obviously stupid and unreasonable.

(b) This is because, in the ordinary down-to-earth areas of life, we know pretty well how we ought to think about what to do. We know that, if we want to find out the best way of getting to some place, we ought to look at the map and try to work it out. But in morals and religion we don't know; and because we don't know, the whole business of trying to think about them becomes far more difficult. In fact it seems to us so difficult that we use or invent various institutions and methods to do our thinking *for* us: 'the Church', 'conscience', 'fashion', 'intuition' and so forth. These are some of the 'respectable' alternatives to thinking: they look respectable, because they are used by all the very many people who can't face the idea of thinking for themselves. It's plain enough that they aren't really respectable, any more than consulting tea-leaves or witch-doctors or visions were really respectable in the past: but they *look* respectable in our society.

(c) What is common to all these escapes from thinking is that *they give people a quick answer*. Human beings want 'the answer' to morals, or religion, or problems of life: perhaps because they are unhappy, or curious, or need to feel secure. They can't face working out the answers for themselves, so they use these escape-methods. The escape-methods won't, of course, give them *right* answers, but at least they give them quick answers, and people can always pretend that they are right, or not bother to think about whether they are right or not.

(d) In particular, the escape-methods don't work because they try to give *the* answer, when there's no such thing. We know this quite well from our ordinary problems, but forget it when it comes to these more difficult ones. For instance, it would obviously be silly to ask for 'the' answer to how to run a farm well, or how to govern the country, or how to play tennis. Thus, running a farm well means knowing about lots of *different* things – the market price for beef, how particular crops and trees grow, how to manage the farm-hands, and so on. There is no single answer: there is no one set of absolute laws or rules which we only have to learn by heart in order to run the farm well. There are a number of very different things: hard facts about what will grow where, attitudes like having a real concern for the farm, skills like knowing how to manage horses or shear sheep, and so on. Only a fool would think that there was such a thing as 'the' answer. And it's even more silly to think this when it comes to things which are clearly more complex and difficult, like how to live well, or how to find 'a meaning for life'. So the first step is to give up asking for 'the answer', or 'the key to life': to give up imagining that there must be some single magic elixir, or some single principle that will make everything clear. It's going to be more a matter of sorting out all the many different things that are relevant into proper categories: of identifying them and finding out how to learn and teach them.

What we have now to do is to try to make clearer some of these apparently 'respectable' ways of finding the answer, so that we can more easily catch ourselves out when we use them to escape the necessity for thinking. Below I have put down some of the more common ones ·that people use. These things are not bad in themselves, and indeed often good. But they are not good *as substitutes* for thinking.

1. *Authority*

(i) *Obeying*. One easy escape from thinking is to stop thinking and do something else – namely, *obey*. Obeying is, for many people, psychologically easier than thinking: just as it's rather relaxing, in a way, to be in the army where you're told what to do and just go ahead and do it, instead of having to make up your own mind. Some people find relief from thinking in obeying a boss, or their husbands or wives, or the commands of some leader-figure (Churchill, or Hitler, or Mao-Tse tung) or the biggest boy in the gang: others have some kind of God whom they obey and whose will they try to do. All this is rather like children obeying their parents. Often they may obey a book of rules (the Bible, the sayings of Mao) laid down by the authority, which comes to much the same thing.

(ii) *Rebelling*. This is like obeying, only the opposite. Some people, instead of deliberately acting in a certain way because some authority wants them to, deliberately act in the opposite way just because some authority doesn't want them to. Such people are just as much obsessed with authority as those who obey, like children who disobey their parents simply in order to show their independence. Young people who need to prove to themselves that they are independent often behave like this: they break rules and conventions, not because they really think in each particular case that this is the reasonable thing to do, but to show to themselves and to the outside world that they are not going to do things just because someone tells them to. This is understandable, but again it's no substitute for thinking about what is the right or reasonable thing to do.

2. 'Ideal People'
Another easy escape is to get hold of some ideal person – somebody you admire – and try to imitate him. (This, too, is rather like what children do with their parents.) Some people admire saint-like people – St Francis, Albert Schweitzer, Gandhi; others have stronger heroes like Churchill, or Lenin; others again admire more obvious heroic achievements, like those of Edmund Hillary or Scott or Francis Chichester; others admire heroic reformers, like Dr Arnold or Florence Nightingale; others admire film or TV stars, or pop singers, or football players, or just people who are strong or handsome or rich and successful. Here too, there is nothing wrong with admiring the right people: but you have to be sure that they *are* the right people, and this means thinking.

3. 'Purpose' and 'Meaning'
Quite a lot of people have some belief, not so much in a personal God to obey or imitate, but in some 'spirit of the universe', 'life-force', 'divine law' or whatever. They talk as if the universe was almost a person: 'the *purpose* of the universe is . . .', 'human beings were *meant* to be . . .', and so forth. This is like a watered-down religion, and is used like a religion to avoid thinking about what one really ought to be or do. Having this picture helps people to feel that the 'answer' to life is something *given* or *laid down*, not something which people can choose, sensibly or unreasonably, for themselves.

4. 'Special experiences'
Many people put their money on some kind of 'special' experience which they take as having some sort of importance or authority. A good example, but one which is not regarded as very 'respectable' nowadays, is 'seeing a vision'. 'Hearing a voice', as Joan of Arc is supposed to have done, is another. Nowadays people talk

more of 'what my conscience tells me', 'my intuition', or say 'I just somehow feel that . . .'. Or they say things like, 'When a man is near death, then he *knows*', or, 'When you're alone with Nature, somehow you can *see* that . . .'. Of course experiences of all kinds are useful and important but we have to think in order to evaluate them. (To put it in religious language, a 'voice' may be from God or the devil.)

5. *'Faith'*

Another reaction – another way of defending ourselves against thinking – is to say things like 'Reason can only get you so far; after that you have to make the leap of faith', or 'You have to rely on intuition'. This is really only a rather stronger version of the last defence we looked at. It says, in effect, that just because you believe something, that by itself makes what you believe right or true. A lot of words, like 'faith', or 'revelation', or 'intuition', are used to cover up this idea, which in its naked form is obviously silly; and there are a great many occasions on which people say things like 'Well, you may argue as much as you like, but I just *know* that . . .'. What is missing here is the notion of *giving reasons* for beliefs. If we abandon this notion, there is really nothing to distinguish sane human beings from lunatics. What makes a lunatic is that he believes something but has no good reason for believing it. To be willing to give reasons, to have your beliefs out in public, to allow them to be inspected and challenged, is essential for all kinds of thinking.

6. *'A matter of taste'*

Then there are those who give up thinking in a way which is becoming increasingly respectable nowadays. They talk as if there are no reasonable principles or standards at all: 'It's all a matter of taste'. They believe, in effect, what suits them (or what they think suits them), and have no desire to think about whether what they believe is *right* or *true*. These people are governed, not by any authority, ideal, etc., but simply by their own mental state, by what they find easiest to believe, or by their own particular desires and feelings. Such people really mean, 'The whole thing is so difficult, I just can't face finding out what's right, so let's drop the subject'.

7. *'How you've been brought up'*

Yet another defence is to say something like, 'Well, it all depends what you've been brought up to believe, doesn't it?', the idea being that if, for instance, you've been brought up to believe that there is a God, or that sleeping with people before you're married is wrong, that settles it; there isn't any need to think about it. But of course, although obviously how you've been brought up does in fact make a great difference to what you believe, it doesn't give you good *reasons* for believing it. If some Nazi who'd been brought up to kill Jews said, 'Well, I was brought up that way, there's no point our arguing about it', we shouldn't accept this as a defence. Indeed, we should think that he was doubly wrong: first, he was wrong about how to treat Jews, and second – which is really far worse – he isn't open to argument. He's resigned from being a reasonable human being; he's no longer open to criticism, or able to change his mind. He is not very far from being mad.

8. *Other People*

A great many people take the 'answers to life' for granted by doing and thinking what their friends do and think. Nearly everybody has some group of people whom he accepts and by whom he is accepted (what sociologists call a 'peer-group'): usually people of the same social class, with similar outlooks and pursuits. They assume that what these people think, and how they act, is right; or if not right, at least not seriously wrong. Phrases like 'decent people', 'right-thinking people', 'properly brought-up people' and so on are used here. The thoughts and actions of the peer-group vary from group to group: they may include fox-hunting or listening to pop music, disliking Negroes or accepting them, having long or short hair, using this or that accent and vocabulary, and having this or that set of manners and conventions. Note that the peer-group may not only actually *set* the standards, i.e. give its individual members ready-made 'answers' to what is right and wrong, but also *reinforce* and *support* the individual's standards. If almost everyone in·the group admire the same 'great man', or obey the same authorities, then not much serious thinking and discussion is likely to get done.

How can we in practice catch ourselves out when we use some of the escapes mentioned above? One way is to cultivate the habit of listening to yourself as you talk. If you can do this, you can catch yourself using words and phrases which are symptomatic of one or other of these escapes. For instance, if you catch yourself talking about 'the meaning of life', 'divine law', 'what God meant us to be' and other such phrases, then you can become aware that you are looking for 'the answer' in an illegitimate way. Similarly, if you find yourself using phrases like 'It's just a matter of taste', 'There is no such thing as right and wrong', 'It is all a matter of how you've been brought up', 'The whole thing is too difficult' or 'I'm not clever enough to think about this sort of thing', then you can become aware that you have decided to chuck up the whole business of thinking altogether. Again. if you say things like, 'Well, none of my friends would do that sort of thing', or 'My parents would not approve', then you will realize that you're just using what other people do as something to imitate and not thinking at all.

Another way is to try and catch yourself before you actually say anything at all. This involves noticing the kinds of things you worry about, and the kinds of ways in which these worries emerge. For instance, you may be the sort of person that worries about what your friends think, or about what is conventional, or about what other people expect of you; and then you can guard against making the mistake of using your friends or convention or other people to do your thinking for you, even before you actually think anything. Or again, if you find yourself wanting to admire a particular person – say Churchill or Hitler or anybody else you like – then you are probably going to use this admiration to do something which you hadn't necessarily thought out. Or you may find yourself having other kinds of worries which are less obvious. You may feel guilty about certain things or worried about your security or social status or whether you find life boring or anxious in certain ways. If you do, you will be likely to adopt some metaphysical or religious outlook on life which (you can pretend) will solve these problems for you. Thus, you may feel that you are guilty or sinful, and adopt a religion according to which if you repent or behave in certain ways you need not feel guilty any more.

The best thing is to make use of a friend to show you yourself, as it were, in a mirror. You can ask him to say honestly whether you are using any of these methods of escape or whether you use the phrases or have the worries which are symptomatic of them. This is just one way of showing yourself to yourself, and any objective method is better than none. If you have no other person there, it may even be useful to switch on a tape recorder and speak your thought aloud into it and then play it back to yourself, so that you can see what you have said. If somebody could invent a cheap machine that took films of you as well as just a recording of your voice, that would be better still.

In general, then, as you will see, thinking is primarily a matter of not just acting and talking, but taking a step backwards and considering in more detail what you do and what you say. If you have not tried it already, you have to be warned not only that it is difficult, but also that it imposes quite a severe strain on anybody. This is nothing to do with how clever you are. It is more a matter of its being so psychologically strenuous that nobody can do it except for short periods at a time. But there is a brighter side: and that is, that once you have made a proper start on the business of thinking, it gets progressively easier, and not only easier, but more enjoyable. You soon come to see that trying to solve these problems, trying to make sense of life, is much more interesting and worthwhile than just living at random, or living a life restricted by some narrow code or creed which you have accepted uncritically. This is part of what Socrates – one of the

first people to think seriously about morals – meant by saying that
'for human beings, the unexamined life is not worth living'.

C. WHAT THINKING INVOLVES
A person who seriously wants to think will find that he needs
three things:
1. *A respect for language.* He will have to make sure that he
   thinks clearly; and since thinking is done in words, this means
   that he must be clear about the meaning of the words he uses.
2. *A respect for fact.* He must be able to find out the facts and
   face them, as opposed to merely hoping that the facts are
   what he wants them to be, or inventing them for his own
   purposes.
3. *A respect for established branches of knowledge.* Scholars and
   research workers have been working away at many of the
   problems which are relevant to morality, religion, and 'the
   meaning of life' for many years. Among the most important
   of these established branches of knowledge are philosophy,
   psychology, sociology, and history. These and others deal with
   human beings and their problems. Anyone who wants to
   think seriously must have some knowledge of these, or at least
   be aware of their importance.

(a) *Methods and Virtues*
If a person is seriously going to try to think for himself, he will
need respect for these three things. But how can he set about
learning to think? What general methods will he use? And what
virtues in himself will he try to cultivate?

It should already be plain that the business of thinking is best
done *in public*, that is to say, in the process of discussion, cross-
questioning, arguing, giving reasons, and so forth. This is because
being reasonable, or thinking correctly, is a public matter and not
a private one: it must stand up to public inspection. It's no good
saying, 'Well, I have my own ideas on this, and my own feelings,
and that's good enough for me'. If it's really good enough for

you, then it must be capable of being shown to other people. It's true that some ways of life or some beliefs may suit certain people, and not suit others, just as some drugs may benefit some men and harm others. But it's also true that you can be right or wrong about what beliefs suit your particular temperament, just as you can be right or wrong about what drugs suit your body, and this makes it a public matter, not just a matter of taste.

Even when you think on your own, or when you're reading a book, you're really conducting a sort of cross-talk with yourself or with the author of the book. If you have any kind of problem which you're trying to solve, you say to yourself something like, 'Well, there's this point, but then again, what about that one? Now supposing this were true, what difference would it make? But is there any evidence that it is true? Let's look at it from another angle: suppose . . .' and so on. This is like what goes on when a group of people discuss something, and it goes on in your own head when you're thinking by yourself. Thinking and talking, or expressing yourself, are very closely connected.

It isn't surprising, then, that most of our weaknesses in thinking come out most obviously when we're discussing with other people. Some people are so nervous or frightened of making fools of themselves that they stay silent, and don't dare to express themselves. Other people are so keen on their own views that they keep repeating them over and over again, without listening to the views of other people. Some people interrupt when others are talking; other people get angry if their opinions are challenged, and turn the discussion into a row. Some people are over-cautious, and try to be absolutely sure that they're right before they say anything; other people are rash, and just charge ahead with their ideas before they've got them properly sorted out. And all of us, above all, need a great deal of practice. It takes young children quite a few years to learn to talk at all, and when we are older, not many of us get to the stage where we can talk properly – where we can conduct a rational conversation, which is more than just gossip or a conventional chat and also which isn't a slanging match.

Teaching people to talk and think is one of the most important things that parents and schools ought to do, and I'm afraid that they don't always do it very well, so that people lack the necessary practice. Because people aren't used to it, they don't realize that it's one of the most exciting and interesting activities there are. They are not very good at thinking, and thinking is quite difficult anyway, so they more or less give up trying. They have a few rather sketchy views about life, or God, or politics, or morals, or marriage, which they've learnt either by taking them direct from their parents, or by reacting violently against their parents; they have not had them submitted to any real questioning or criticism. As they get older, they get less and less inclined to think, and begin more and more to act and talk like robots or puppets, just going through the motions of life without really questioning and examining the world around them. Sometimes one feels that they might as well be dead, and this is rather frightening.

Thinking is not really an *intellectually* difficult thing to do. You don't require a very high I.Q., or need to know a vast number of facts. It's a skill, like learning to walk or to swim or to play a game. What you need is patience, and plenty of practice. You have got to try to be *workmanlike*: it's no good being high-minded, or just talking vaguely in a rather grand way. Thinking is a job like any other: treat it with the seriousness and down-to-earth common sense that is appropriate to doing a job well.

(b) *The Different Disciplines*
You don't have to think for long before realizing that you can think about different *kinds* of questions: and these come under the different disciplines. Thus there are questions in science, questions in mathematics, questions in history, and so on: and there are experts in all these and other fields.

Problems about morals and religion and life in general are particularly difficult, because most people don't understand the different kinds of questions that arise, and don't know about the different disciplines that deal with them. There are questions about *meaning* and *concepts* (philosophy), questions about the individual human mind (psychology), and questions about human behaviour in social groups (sociology). Philosophy does not deal with facts, but with meaning and concepts: psychology and sociology deal with facts, but with special kinds of facts about human beings.

Nearly all questions about life in general have to be broken down into a number of questions which fall within one or more of these disciplines. It would take too long to explain the disciplines here, but I should like to stress that nobody could regard himself as seriously concerned with questions about morals, religion and life unless he was also seriously concerned with these disciplines. To try to decide how men ought to live without taking philosophy and psychology and sociology into account is rather like deciding how to build an aeroplane without taking mathematics or science into account.

Of course there are other areas of study also which are relevant. By learning history, or reading some of the best novels, a person can acquire a good deal of experience and understanding about how human beings behave: and this is very important, if the disciplines mentioned above are not to become too dry, or abstract, or removed from basic human experience. A genuine understanding of how men of another historical period thought and acted, or of characters portrayed by novelists, is of great value: though we must take care that we do not read them simply for entertainment or amusement, but rather to learn something.

(c) *Books*

Books by themselves aren't much good. There's as much resistance to them – and for the same reasons – as there is to thinking. Somebody can read a book and say, 'Well, that's quite interesting', and it may have had no effect on him whatsoever. This is because he hasn't had to do any work himself; he has read the words, but perhaps hasn't bothered to think about them – to criticize them, argue about them, and so on. If you don't do this, books are a bore, and this is probably why so few people read them. But a book can help as a starting-off point – so long as the author doesn't try to do your thinking *for* you, but simply tries to *make* you think. This isn't easy, and the author is often tempted to do too much: to give you too much of his views, and express himself at too great a length. After that – indeed, I hope, during it as well – you need to argue amongst yourselves and with other people. It helps to make yourself write things down, because by doing this you can gain a clear idea of what you really think, and then you can show it to somebody who will criticize it for you, and help you to get clearer. There is of course a great deal written about all these subjects, and at the end I've put a list of books which it would be useful to read. But there would be no point in doing this unless you have already acquired the habit of thinking and arguing. You've got to want to know before you have any chance of finding out. You've got to be able to tolerate doubt, and uncertainty, and not being sure whether you're right, and you've got to learn to take and give criticism in public.

two

The Basic Rules

A. RULES AND FRAMEWORKS

In the last chapter (p. 6) we talked about obedience or dis-obedience to authority, or a set of imposed rules, as one substitute for thinking. So it is plain enough that the rules and authorities in a school, or any other institution, or in society generally, are not to be regarded as ends in themselves. They are not there by divine right, so to speak, or just because the authorities are powerful and can make people obey. For it must always be possible to question the rules or the authorities, to think about whether they are right or wrong. To put it another way: getting people to think, to make up their own minds reasonably, comes first; and the function of rules and authorities must be subordinated to this end.

Very roughly, this is what we might mean by a liberal society as opposed to a totalitarian or dictatorial one. People sometimes think that a liberal society means one in which you can do as you like, whereas in a totalitarian society you do what you're told. But in fact, all societies have rules and authorities: the real difference is in what the function of the rules and authorities is supposed to be. In liberal societies the function is to give people freedom and security so that they can think for themselves; in totalitarian ones the rules and authorities make up the individual's mind for him – he is not supposed to think or question, but just to obey the rules or be indoctrinated into whatever the authorities think is best for him (or for them). What we object to in totalitarian societies, like Nazi Germany, is not just that they had bad rules and bad authorities: much more important is that they felt they had the right to tell people what to think. They used rules and authorities to produce the sort of people with the sort of beliefs they wanted.

Rules are inevitable

But once we understand this, another thing becomes obvious: and that is, that what rules and authorities you have is just as important for liberal societies as for totalitarian ones. You can't help people to think, or educate them, or bring them up to be free and reasonable, just by leaving them alone and having no rules at all. People sometimes talk as if anything you could call a 'rule' must somehow be a wicked thing imposed by some tyrannical authority. But in fact without following rules we would not be human beings at all. Rules are needed to play games, do business, drive cars, arrange for people to be fed and housed, and for every other human activity. What distinguishes human beings from animals is that human beings are rule-following creatures. You can't think or talk without following rules, the rules of language. A child who was never taught the rules of language wouldn't grow up to be human.

Every child, and every adult too, needs a framework and a set of rules. It's not just that he feels more secure in such a framework, though (particularly for young children) that is also true: it is rather that without such a framework, he will never learn anything. For instance, if we want to teach something to two children in a primary school, we can't even begin to do this if they are fighting, or not listening, or drunk, or suffering terribly from toothache. We have to arrange for certain *preconditions* for educating people to be established: in particular, we have to arrange things so that they can communicate with each other and learn from other people.

This is very much like the rules needed to make the methods of even the most liberal society work at all. A primitive society might settle its disputes by fighting, so that the strongest party wins: then perhaps we make progress, and agree to talk things over by means of a discussion or a parliamentary debate. But this at once means that we have to have rules: you can't have a discussion or a debate if people are throwing spears at each other. Indeed the rules you need to follow in order to get a good discussion or debate are quite complicated: it doesn't work well if people insult or shout at each other, or just hurl abuse, or keep interrupting. You need rules of procedure. You also, of course, have to make sure that people are not too ill or upset to discuss things: that they are adequately defended against their external enemies: that they have had enough to eat, and so forth.

Rules have a purpose
We have to remember, then, that rules are supposed to have a point or purpose – to make a better game, to get a proper discussion, or whatever. Of course some rules may not have much point, and can be scrapped; other rules may be very important and well-suited to what we are trying to do; others again may need some improvement or additions. It all depends on what we are out to achieve. We have to have one kind of rule for a company of soldiers in battle, another for a cricket team, and another for a class-room discussion or a parliamentary debate. None of these have to be 'moral' rules, if by that is meant that we look on them as ideally right or good in themselves. It is just that they serve particular human needs or wants or interests.

This is why both the notion of total conformity and the notion of total anarchy are logically absurd for human beings. For (i) if people always obeyed the rules, never questioning them but simply going through the patterns of behaviour which the rules prescribed, we would not be able to distinguish them from animals governed entirely by their instincts – like birds building nests, or ants or bees. It is part of the concept of a human being that he is capable of not conforming – that if he follows rules, then to some extent he does so deliberately and of his own free will. But equally (ii), and for similar reasons, anarchy is impossible for human beings. For to be human means, at least, that one learns to talk and think by conforming to the rules governing language and meaning; and apart from this basic consideration, anything which we could properly·call a *society* would involve a number of human beings making some kind of contracts with each other – and contracts are a form of rule-keeping. Those who call themselves 'anarchists' are usually protesting (whether they know it or not) against *particular* authorities or *particular* kinds of rules, not against having any rules at all.

All this means that what sort of rules we ought to have, in particular contexts and for particular purposes, is a very open question, which can often only be settled by finding out more facts than we know already. For instance, it is pretty obvious that for many (perhaps all) purposes, we need to have rules about telling the truth, keeping promises, and not hurting or killing people. It would be hard to see how any communal activity could flourish if we did not, for the most part, abide by such rules: though of course we may make exceptions in special cases. But there will be plenty of other cases where we are not sure whether we need rules in a certain area or not, or not sure about what actual rules to have.

For example, we might agree that for the purposes of having an efficient army we had to subject the soldiers to certain disciplinary regulations. Obviously one rule must be that they obey their officers. But what about making them keep their uniforms clean, and drill on the parade ground? Some would argue that this is a waste of time, and that their efficiency as a fighting force would not be impaired – or might even be improved – if there were no rules in this area. Others might claim that cleanliness of uniform and drill contributed to efficiency. In fact, of course, we cannot be sure of the answer to this; we might have to rely on guesswork and the collective experience of army officers. But we would try to settle the question, not by saying (i) that soldiers *just ought* to conform to these rules, nor by saying (ii) that the rules were *just silly* traditions or conventions which ought to be scrapped at once. We would settle the question on the evidence, and try to find out whether or not such rules contributed to the purposes which we wished to achieve.

Again, we might agree that at a university or college the purpose of having the students there was so that they might learn certain subjects efficiently. So it would obviously be necessary to have rules of some kind or other which ensured that they worked reasonably hard, read the right books, turned up for lectures, or whatever was thought essential to the purpose of learning. Similarly, if students who became addicted to certain drugs were consequently unable to learn properly, we should have rules banning such addiction. But what about rules governing their 'private lives' – for instance, rules about sexual behaviour or dress? Here too we must not be doctrinaire: we must not say, with unthinking conformity, that they just ought to keep certain rules because this produces 'decent behaviour' or 'proper manners'; but nor must we say, with an over-hasty rebelliousness, that the rules are certainly irrelevant to the purpose. It might be the case that certain types of sexual behaviour affect the student's ability to learn – for good or ill; or it might be the case that they make no difference.

B. CONTRACTS AND DECISION-PROCEDURES

Young children are not, in general, capable of making up their own rules in a sensible way; indeed, they are not capable of understanding the kind of considerations mentioned above. They would not be able to understand them, unless we made them follow certain rules in the first place; for only so could they come to grasp the whole idea of rules and the purposes of rules. So in effect parents and teachers *initiate* children into certain contexts which are governed by rules, in the hope that when they are older and have learnt more about the world they will be able to make up their own minds in a reasonable way. We give children more and more freedom as they get older, until when they are adult we allow them to choose their own way of life for themselves.

Naturally there are difficulties about the particular point at which it seems right to consider children as 'grown up'. But in general, we feel that we have some kind of mandate or right to supervise young children: we do not regard them as completely free and responsible agents, so we curtail their liberty; and in return we look after them – feed, house, clothe and protect them, give them education and guidance, and so forth. At some time – perhaps at the school-leaving age, when they can be economically independent if they wish – we give up this mandate. Thereafter we hope that they may wish to continue being educated, and will want to learn from other people in our society; but we cannot enforce this. This is the position that applies, in some degree at least, to sixth-formers, university and college students, and so forth.

But when the child or adolescent is considered to be adult, and has become free of the particular rules which parents and teachers imposed upon him, he does not thereby become free of all rules. It is in principle possible that he may be able to live entirely by himself on a desert island, owing nothing to and being owed nothing by any other person; but even this is in practice impossible (all desert islands belong to somebody nowadays). In fact he will go to college, or do a job, or at any rate exist as a member of some sovereign state – Great Britain, or France, or somewhere else. Unlike the young child, he can opt for one out of a number of possibilities: he doesn't *have* to go to college, if he doesn't like Britain he can emigrate, and so on. But he will certainly find himself within some rule-governed situation or other.

This means that, in effect, he enters more or less consciously and deliberately into some kind of *contract*. This may not be an obvious and ordinary contract, such as that between a worker and an employer, or one businessman and another; but it will be a contract just the same. It is helpful here to think of choosing a contract in the light of choosing whether to play a particular game. By choosing to play cricket, or bridge, or anything else, one contracts to obey a particular set of rules in common with other people. Often the rules do not cover every possible contingency, so that there are authorities empowered to interpret them, like umpires in cricket and referees in football; and part of the contract is that the players are supposed to accept the umpire's or referee's ruling – he is, so to speak, part of the rules of the game. In just the same way, in any society, there will be rules (sometimes in the form of constitutions) and authorities: chairmen, parliaments, vice-chancellors, headmasters, committees and so forth.

Of course these contracts work both ways: the contractor not only is obliged to obey the rules, but also is entitled to receive benefits under the rules. For instance, part of the contract in this country is that citizens pay income tax, the money from which is spent on things like roads, education, a health service and so on, which are of use to those citizens. At a university, students agree to obey the rules about lectures, reading books, etc., and receive in return the teaching and opportunities for learning which the university provides. In the army, soldiers accept military law, in return for which the army clothes, feeds and in general looks after the soldiers.

Rules about changing rules
However, as we have seen, rules and contracts which embody rules can be changed. In order to make a change, we need some kind of *decision-procedure*; that is, some kind of agreement about legitimate and illegitimate ways of changing the rules. Thus if we were forming a social club, or a small society on a desert island, we should probably think something like this: 'Well, let's have such-and-such rules for the time being, since these seem the most sensible ones: but maybe we shall want to change them in the future. Now what shall we do – shall we elect a boss who can change the rules when he wants, or a small committee of three people who can change them? Or shall we say that everybody must vote, and that the rules can only be changed if there is a majority of more than 50 per cent? Or should we require a two-thirds majority? Or what?' In coming thus to agree about what ways of changing the rules we *were* going to allow, we should also be agreeing about what ways we were *not* going to allow. For instance, we should probably say, 'We'll discuss changes in the rules, but people mustn't keep shouting or fighting during the

discussions. We will allow people to make speeches, or carry banners with slogans, but we won't allow them to throw bricks or spears', and so forth.

So here we have, not just agreement about the ordinary rules, but agreement about rules-about-changing-rules, rules about decision-procedures. In any large society this usually means some agreement about the 'sovereign body', the ultimate court of appeal; in this country Parliament is normally taken to be sovereign, but in other countries ·it might be a particular oligarchy, or a dictator, or the will of the people as expressed in a vote or referendum. And there will also be rules, more or less clearly stated, about what is allowable by way of trying to change the rules: putting pressure on a Member of Parliament, or peaceful demonstration, or speaking in Hyde Park, are all legitimate; throwing bombs or assassinating Prime Ministers are not.

All this is going to apply to any society, any contractual situation or 'game' played in common: even to a small society of two members, as with a married couple. We may hope, of course, that it may not be necessary to spell out all the rules all the time: in marriage, for instance, the couple may get on together so well that they need not bother to keep thinking about their contractual obligations or decision-procedures. But on the other hand, if there is any trouble or difficulty, we are inevitably thrown back on some such agreement. The only alternative to such agreement is for a person to opt out of that particular society altogether.

Putting up with rules

It is not likely that we shall be able to offer every individual exactly the sort of 'game' or contract which he likes. I might prefer to have the rules of cricket changed, so that I'm not obliged to spend long and boring hours fielding rather than batting; but if I can't get them changed, then either I must play cricket and put up with having to field, or else I can't play cricket. Similarly, in any contract or society, there will probably be things which I dislike, or of which I morally disapprove, or which I regard as irrational, tiresome, silly, scandalous or wicked. Naturally I will try to get these changed, but if I want to join the society at all, then (i) I am obliged to keep the rules in the meantime, and (ii) I am obliged to restrict myself to allowable methods of getting the rules changed, since the rules about what methods are allowable are themselves amongst the rules I contract for.

Thus if you are born and brought up in England, you are faced with a choice. By remaining part of the system, you get whatever advantages the system has – such things as a health service, national assistance if you're out of work, free education, law and order, and so forth. You have the right to try to change any rules you disapprove of by certain methods. On the other hand, you have to keep the rules which permit these advantages – paying income tax, not stealing, etc. – and the rules which disallow certain methods of change, such as using violence on other people or setting fire to buildings. Thus you are not obliged to believe that all the rules are particularly good rules, or that the values enshrined in English society are the right ones, but you are obliged to play the game according to the rules. You can either accept this contractual obligation if you think it is worth your while, or else you can refuse and emigrate.

All this would remain true in any situation or society. But this is not to say that the rules we have in any society are good ones. In particular, we may think that the rules about decision-procedures, and the general structure of many societies, are very unsatisfactory in that they do not allow enough people to participate in making decisions enough of the time. Situations develop in which society gets divided into 'we', who are on the receiving end of the rules, and 'they' who make the rules. Workers, students and others feel that the rules are not *their* rules. Of course, even if they are not, they still have to decide whether to contract for them or to opt out of society altogether: but it is quite understandable that they feel left out of the most important part of the game, that is, left out of making up and changing the rules. There is a lot to be said about how to make societies more democratic, bring more people into the game, and hence avoid

these difficulties, and it is very important that particular societies
– not only countries like England, but also smaller societies like
universities and schools – should devote a good deal of thought to
this: but this question is not relevant to our present purpose.

Rules must be clear

We may end by noting one point, however. When such difficulties arise, a good deal of the trouble is caused by *lack of clarity
about the contract*. For instance, to take a topical case, the
university authorities may have a very vaguely-stated expectation
that the students will 'behave reasonably' or 'not bring the university into disrepute'. But this might be interpreted quite differ-
ently, in practice, by the authorities and the students. If what was
meant by 'behaving reasonably' were clearly spelled out, and the
students asked either to contract for this or else not to come to the
university, we could avoid trouble. So too with other situations:
trouble arises partly because it is just *not clear what the rules are*.
If everyone shares common values and ways of behaving, this
doesn't matter much, but we live in a time when this is not true,
and the only thing is to get both parties to state clearly what rules
they want to contract for.

This is something which students, workers and others who
often feel that rules are just authoritarian impositions can try to
achieve. Too often we see authorities trying simply to maintain
their authority without clarity about rules and without any clear
views about what changes are required. There are vested interests
on both sides: the authorities may mask theirs by talking about
'law and order', 'decent behaviour' and so forth; and the under-
dogs may deceive themselves that they are acting out of idealism,
reformist zeal, etc. A greater understanding of what has been
pointed out above would help both sides.

*   *   *

The point of a proper understanding of the above considerations
is not just that it is nice to be clear. It is rather that the whole

business of deciding what to do, learning to think, and making reasonable judgements about morality, religion and other difficult areas of life, is at present made very much harder because it is confused with the doctrinaire attitudes to rules that we have mentioned. A person who feels compelled to conform, or compelled to rebel, has little time and less energy to go about the business of thinking at all. In particular, morality and moral issues become confused with whether we are going to obey or disobey; whereas, as we shall see, this is not a proper description of the area of morality at all. To this we shall turn in the next chapter; and if we can avoid wasting too much energy on emotional reactions to rules, we may be able to think about morality to greater effect.

three

What Morals are About

In Chapter One we outlined some of the ways in which people tried to escape from the business of thinking; and it will be helpful to remember these when we try to answer the first question, which will naturally be something like, 'What *are* "morals" anyway? What's a moral issue, or a moral belief, as against other kinds of issues or beliefs – scientific beliefs, for instance? What sort of a subject is "morals" and how do you do it?' Deciding what morals are, and deciding what to do in particular moral situations, both involve a kind of thinking: and that knocks out all the escape-routes we noticed in Chapter One. People who simply conform, or rebel, or follow their impulses, or imitate other people, or 'have faith', aren't thinking or deciding at all.

Some of these escape-routes are so popular that they get turned into *theories* about morals: and there are two general theories, or collections of theories, which are still quite popular. I think they are certainly wrong, but people tend to fall back on them for lack of anything better.

(1) There is the view that, when people call things morally right or wrong, they are only expressing their own prejudices or tastes, or saying that they like or dislike such things, or trying to arouse sentiments of like or dislike in other people. On this view moral judgements aren't really *judgements* at all: they don't set out to say what is really right or true or reasonable, but merely reflect the speaker's own feelings.

(2) There is the view that some things really are right or wrong,

and can be known to be so: but that we get to know what's right and wrong by some kind of intuition, or revelation, or special perception or feeling (perhaps 'conscience'), which simply *tells* us the answer. On this view we don't have to find out what's right and wrong, we somehow *see* it, rather as we might just see that things are red or square.

What's wrong with the first view (1) is that when we call things good or bad, right or wrong, we obviously aren't just expressing our feelings. It isn't just that we dislike or feel strongly about Hitler killing millions of Jews: we think there is something really wrong with it, which would still be wrong even if we didn't have any particular feelings about it at all. Words like 'good' and 'right' have more to them than phrases such as 'I like it', 'That makes me feel better', etc. What's wrong with the second view (2) is that calling things good or bad, right or wrong, obviously isn't exactly the same as stating facts: it's also to set some kind of *value* on the facts. 'Good' and 'right' aren't the same as fact-words like 'red' and 'square': we use 'good' and 'right' to commend, approve, prescribe behaviour, influence choices and so on, not just to describe things. We may be able to find out that some things are really good or bad, but we can't just *see* them to be so. What both these views miss out – significantly, because it means hard work – is any notion of *reasons* for saying that things are good or bad, right or wrong. According to (1), things aren't really good or bad anyway, so there can't be any reasons at all: according to (2), you just somehow see things to be good or bad, and don't really need reasons at all.

A. THE IMPORTANCE OF REASONS

We need to remember, then, that whatever moral thought and action are they must rely on *some* kind of reasons. Very often, indeed, when people say and do things (whether in the area of morality or not), they don't have reasons: they just say the first thing that comes into their head, or act on impulse. But this sort of behaviour, as we saw in the previous chapter, is not really human: it is to behave more like animals – talking parrots or busy ants. Human beings follow rules and have reasons. It's worth while explaining more fully how this is relevant to morality:

1. *Reasons and intentions*

The essential point to understand here is that such concepts as 'telling the truth', 'keeping a promise', 'stealing', 'being kind', etc. *involve more than just a set of noises or physical movements.* They involve also the notions of *intention*, of *understanding*, and *knowing what you are doing.* The general importance of these can be grasped most quickly if we ask ourselves why animals, or machines, or infants cannot tell the truth, or keep promises, or steal, or be kind or cruel. A parrot might say, 'It's a fine day' when it was a fine day, or when it wasn't: but it would not be telling the truth or lying. You could build a robot to say, 'I promise to be here when you come back', and it might be there when you came back : but it would not have made or kept a promise. I put sixpence in a ticket machine, and it doesn't give me a ticket but just takes the money, I couldn't say it had *stolen* it, except as a sort of joke. It is significant that the joke would really consist of regarding the machine as if it were a person, as if there were a little man inside.

People can do these things because they know what they are doing. They don't just go through the motions: they *act intentionally*. Similarly, they don't just make noises that happen to be words: they *speak meaningfully*. Moral words are all tied down, in varying degrees, to the notion of intention. You can't murder somebody by mistake, because 'murder' means 'intending to kill'. You can't lie by mistake, because in order to lie you've got to know that you're lying. You can't make a promise entirely by accident, because 'making a promise' entails committing yourself, usually by some form of words (like 'I promise') uttered in a context which you know is regarded as morally binding: if a foreigner said 'I promise', thinking that it meant 'I hope', he might be very stupid or negligent, but he wouldn't have made a promise.

Another way of putting this is in terms of free will. Suppose somebody throws me forcibly against another person, so that my body hits that person and kills him. I have not murdered him, since what happened was not the result of any free choice of mine. Indeed, it would be rather misleading to say, 'I killed him', at least without further explanation, since even the word 'kill' often implies that I did something intentionally, whereas in this case I have, in a sense, done nothing at all: I have merely had my body used as an instrument. We could imagine a series of cases, in which varying degrees of kinds of pressure were put upon me: physical force, hypnotic commands, threats, and so forth. In all these cases, my responsibility is diminished,[1] because I am acting to some extent under duress. The point here is that my *moral* responsibility is diminished, because my responsibility for *what happens* is diminished; what happens is not something that *I* (freely) *do*.

Morality implies freedom

It can be seen from this that if a person is to act morally, he must know what he is doing, and must do it freely – that is, it must really be *he* who does it, and not some form of duress or compulsion that makes him do it. One difficulty with a programme of 'making people behave morally', even in the primitive sense of 'keeping the rules of society', is now apparent. For even in this sense there is a conflict between the idea of *making* or *forcing* (in a very strong sense) somebody to do something, and his doing it *freely* or *intentionally*: and if intentionality is required for moral action, then we cannot make people act morally. For instance, we could in principle devise a machine which paralysed a person's arm if he tried to touch anything that belonged to someone else, or tried to assault someone else: and we might be tempted to say that we had 'made him refrain' from stealing or from assault. But this would only be true in a very weak sense. It is true that he doesn't take the property, but not true that he (deliberately or

---

[1] It is diminished in different degrees by different cases, of course. Physical force abolishes it completely, because it is no longer my action: threats and other forms of duress only diminish it slightly.

intentionally) refrains from taking it: he just doesn't take it – he can't take it.

What we can do, if we want, is to make people go through certain motions, or sets of physical movements, which might *look* like cases of people acting morally. The object of this might be to keep them out of trouble, or to stop them being a nuisance. If I condition a child, by giving it electric shocks, so that it can never shout loudly or bump into other people, then one might be tempted to talk of the child as 'well-behaved'. The same result could be achieved by putting a silencer over its mouth and tying it in a straitjacket. Certainly it is 'well-behaved' in a sense: but in another sense it is not *behaving* or *acting* at all:[1] it has no choice.

2. 'Raw' feelings

If the notion of a moral action demands more than a set of physical movements, so too does it demand more than a set of feelings. Thus moral virtues like 'kindness' or 'honesty' are not reducible to a collection of consistent impulses or psychological promptings. Somebody who is kind to animals is not *simply* somebody who feels impelled to feed cats, angry when horses are ill-treated, or guilty at having to leave his dog in a dog's home. These 'raw' feelings and impulses may *motivate* kind actions, but they are not the whole story. The impulse to feed animals may result in over-feeding them, so that they become ill or die. Here we feel inclined to say that this is not kindness but cruelty. What we should say is that it is neither. A raw feeling which leads to an

---

[1] Here and elsewhere I have deliberately oversimplified the issues, in an endeavour to make the main point as forcibly as possible. It would be more correct to say that words like 'behaving', 'acting', 'doing' (and other verbs with a more specific meaning) are sometimes used in contexts which imply the notion of intentionality, and sometimes not. (One does not require an excuse for talking of 'animal behaviour', or for saying that someone did something (or acted) unintentionally.) Again, if a man (for instance) threatens me with a gun, it is perfectly correct to say that he can 'make me do something', that I choose to do it, and do it intentionally. All I intend to exclude here are those cases which would cut out intention and freedom altogether.

action, may – accidentally, as it were – result in behaviour which we might call 'kind' (just as an electric shock might result in a chess-player making 'the right' move): but kindness is not just the feeling-plus-action. Kindness is an intentional or voluntary disposition: a person who is kind to animals is disposed to act in the animal's interests, and he will follow or check his impulses to feed animals according to those interests.

Similarly, a man may have raw feelings of guilt on certain occasions, e.g. when confronted by customs officers. Sometimes these may correlate with his 'immoral' behaviour, if for instance he is actually smuggling something: but at other times they may not – some people feel guilty even if they aren't smuggling anything at all. To *feel* guilty in itself is no indication of honesty or dishonesty. Morality begins only when the man *thinks* that he ought or ought not to smuggle. He might arrive at either of these beliefs partly as a result of his feeling guilty, but he might also arrive at them as a result of other considerations (such as whether he is damaging the country's economy, whether it will involve him in lying, and so on). He behaves honestly if he is following some rule or acting on some belief, not if he is merely impelled by a feeling of guilt.

3. *Acting for a reason*
It is roughly on these grounds that moral action is tied to the notion of rationality. But we must be careful to understand what is meant by 'rationality' here. Take the case of the person who suddenly brakes his car to avoid a smash. This is a rational action, and the man 'has a reason' for doing it. But it need not be the case that he acted deliberately, in the sense of making a conscious choice, or going through any process of ratiocination: he need not be *thinking about* what he is doing. In a sense, one might say that he did it out of habit, just as he habitually turns on the ignition before pressing the self-starter. Nor has his action got to be a good or sensible one. A motorist might apply the brakes when his car skids, though in fact it might be better if he did not brake, but straightened the wheels instead. But this would still be, in one

sense, a rational action: that is, he would have braked *in order* to stop the car skidding. He would have been following a rule ('when skids, then brake'), even though it would have been a wrong rule.

If people are to act morally at all, therefore, they must act for a reason in this sense: they must not be, so to speak, just pushed around by causes. There is thus a vital distinction between feelings of guilt, repulsion, aversion, taboo, etc. (or strong desires, passions, and impulses) which make people avoid or seek out certain things, and people acting voluntarily, intentionally, and for a reason. If I ask somebody, 'Why don't you eat human flesh?' and he says, 'I just can't swallow it, my revulsion is so great', he has given me an answer, but has said nothing about having moral reasons or any sort of justification. If on the other hand, he says, 'Well, I could eat it, but I think it is wrong to do so, because . . .' then he has given me a rational justification (whether a good or a bad justification does not matter here).

Rational actions, we might say, are those for which the agent is responsible. They are attempts which *we* make (not physical movements forced on us) to meet a particular situation in the external world: the situation of an imminent crash, or of pieces placed on a chess-board, or of people living in a particular relationship or in society at large. Rationality is the characteristically human way of dealing with the world. Consequently we can be had up, so to speak, for dealing with it well or badly. If we are not acting rationally (in this narrow sense), we cannot be had up at all: for it is not *we* who are responsible. We can neither get good marks for good moral behaviour, nor bad marks for bad behaviour.

4. *Rationalizations*

If an action is to fall within the moral sphere, therefore, it must be rational: and this implies that it must be done for a reason. But this means more than that the agent must also in principle be able to say why he did it. It means that the reason must also be causally operative: it must not be a rationalization. Thus a man might never eat human beings, be able to give excellent reasons why eating them was wrong, and think that these reasons were what influenced his behaviour; yet it might still be true that what really stopped him eating people was some unconscious feeling of guilt or taboo. We could indeed say in one sense that what he did, considered by itself, was rational: that is, that reasons could be given for it. But in a more important sense *he* would not be acting rationally.

It is likely that a great deal of our behaviour is rationalized rather than rational, in this sense. To take another example, it may be that there are good biological reasons for not committing incest; but it is not at all clear that these reasons are *our* reasons, except in the sense that we can quote them. One could test this by supposing a situation where it was rationally desirable to mate with one's close relations (perhaps we are the last survivors of the human race), and seeing whether this change in the facts would actually produce a change of behaviour – for if our anti-incest behaviour was rationally motivated, then we would be flexible enough to alter it. In the same way there are pacifists who never fight because, in effect, they are psychologically capable of killing (perhaps they have a deep unconscious dread of shedding blood, or something), and pacifists who never fight because they believe (rightly or wrongly) that no situation could arise in which killing would be justified. Both may give the same account of why they act as they do, but the former would be rationalizing: whereas the latter, if presented with a situation in which killing was justified, would be prepared to kill.[1]

---

[1] The last example shows that the concept of rationality applies to beliefs as well as to actions. A moral belief, like any other belief, must be held *for a reason*: otherwise it is not a belief, but merely a form of words which a person utters: just as an action must be done for a reason, if it is not to be merely a set of physical movements. If we asked somebody, 'Why do you believe so-and-so?' and he said, 'For absolutely no reason at all', we would be thoroughly mystified. Moreover, there is a close connection between the content of a belief and its reasons. Suppose that a person said, 'Birth control is wrong', and gave as his sole reason that his church said so: suppose that the church changes its mind, so that

The degree to which an action or a belief are rational is connected with how far they are really *our own*: that is, how far they are the result of our facing facts and responding freely, rather than compulsively, to them. In so far as our actions approximate to mere reactions or reflex movements, and our beliefs to sets of words which are merely parroted or accepted solely on authority, to that extent we fall away from acting and thinking as moral agents.

B. REASONS AND OTHER PEOPLE'S INTERESTS

Valuing, choosing, commending, etc. are certainly different from stating, describing, or noting facts. But they are not arbitrary activities: they have their own standards of success. Consequently we have to sketch those rules, principles or standards in virtue of which we can say that one moral belief is better than another. The words which we should most naturally use, in making this sort of judgement, would include 'reasonable', 'rational', 'unprejudiced', 'sensible', 'wise' and 'sane'. In this section I shall in fact make most use of the word 'rational', and try to outline the senses in which we can say that one moral belief is more rational than another, or that one person is more rational than another in the sphere of morality.

It is natural to begin by trying to consider what we mean when we call *people*, rather than *beliefs*, rational or irrational. When we describe somebody as 'irrational', 'unreasonable', 'intolerant', 'prejudiced', 'insane', etc. we do not (or should not) refer primarily to the truth or falsehood of his beliefs. A man may hold beliefs which are perfectly correct in an unreasonable, intolerant, prejudiced or insane *manner* – and, of course, vice versa. We are

---

he then goes around saying, 'Birth control is right'. How misleading is it to say that he believes that birth control is wrong, and then that it is right? We might feel tempted to say that what he really believes is that whatever his church says is right. (He might not even know what 'birth control' *meant*.)

talking about the *way in which* or the *reasons for which* he comes to believe, and continues to believe, rather than *what* he believes. A 'reasonable' man is not essentially a man who believes *x*, *y* and *z*, but a man who is prepared to listen to argument, attend to the facts, to logic, to the meanings of words, and so on. We tend to assume that certain beliefs, being so obviously false, could only be held by somebody who was unreasonable or prejudiced or insane: for instance, it seems to most of us that anyone who thought the earth was flat, or that all those of Aryan blood were superior to all non-Aryans, must have failed to attend to the evidence. But we must not be tempted to suppose that it is the belief itself which justifies our charge of unreasonableness. Plenty of inventors and scientists have been thought unreasonable or insane because their views did not find favour at the time: and afterwards they were found to be correct. It is the sort of reasons a man has for his beliefs which count.

To put this another way: We can distinguish the merits of a person when playing a particular role from the correctness or incorrectness of his beliefs. For instance, we can talk about a 'good scientist', meaning (roughly) a person who observes the physical world closely and patiently, who frames hypotheses intelligently and submits them to experimental tests, and who is prepared to abide by the relevant evidence. More obscurely, but still intelligibly, a 'good literary critic' is someone who is widely and deeply read in literature, is well-versed in certain studies which are relevant to literature (perhaps the history of the period, or the life of the author), shows an acute perception of human nature and the literary forms which portray it, and so forth. We can categorize individuals as 'good' at these activities without necessarily maintaining that their scientific or literary opinions are, in any particular case, correct. We mean rather that they are good at following certain rules of procedure, or principles of thought, which are relevant to their fields of study; in much the same way as somebody can be a good bridge-player without necessarily making all his contracts, or a good barrister without winning all his cases.

Being 'good at' morality

What is it, then, to be 'good at' morality? I am suggesting that we ought *not* to try to answer this question by saying, 'Holding the right moral views'. If we say this, we shall find ourselves asking next 'But what *are* the right moral views?'; and to this question we may fail to find an answer. We may fail for two reasons: first, because we don't yet know how to decide which *are* the 'right' moral views: and second, because we still might not know which actual views were right, even if we knew what we meant by calling a view 'right' – we might, for instance, not have enough factual information to decide between conflicting views. We should rather ask, 'What are the rules of procedure, or the principles of relevance, which we actually use to assess the merits of a moral view?', or 'What sort of demands do we make on a person who puts forward a moral view, when we want him to justify it?' I don't think it should worry us too much to realize that, even if and when we have established the rules of procedure for morality, we still cannot in a strict sense *prove* this or that specific moral view to be 'right' beyond any possible doubt.

After all, we are in a not very dissimilar position as regards scientific views. We have a fairly good idea of what rules and criteria govern the activity of science, and how scientific arguments and justifications are supposed to work. But this does not mean that we never hold mistaken scientific beliefs, however careful we try to be in attending to the rules and criteria – we may have overlooked some vital fact, or our instruments may not be good enough to collect all the evidence we need. Nor does it mean that our scientific beliefs can be shown to follow logically from certain pieces of evidence – that they are *necessarily* true. A person can, without actual contradiction, accept all the evidence normally taken to show that the earth is round, and still maintain that it is flat. It would be irrational of him to do so, because he would not be abiding by the rules of procedure which govern scientific activity, but it would not be nonsensical – any more than it would be nonsensical of him to hold a particular moral view, whatever the facts might be. Yet we can still talk about 'proof', 'knowledge', and 'certainty' in science as in logic or mathematics. And so we can in morals. These words will relate to different rules of procedure according to the activity. Different activities have different standards, but this does not mean that one is inferior to another: they are just different.

With some of the rules of procedure in morality we are perfectly familiar, because they are rules which enter into other activities besides morality. Briefly they are:

(a) That we should stick to the laws of logic;
(b) That we should use language correctly;
(c) That we should attend to the facts.

Many examples have been given of these kinds of rationality: they may be found elsewhere, and I will not repeat them here.[1] We all know that if, during a moral argument, a person contradicts himself, or disregards some fact which is relevant to his opinion, or plays fast and loose with the meanings of words, he is behaving irrationally.

What makes a moral opinion

These particular rules of procedure, however, are not peculiar to morality, even though they enter into it. In our search for other rules of procedure, it seems most profitable to begin by one account of a certain type of thinking which has a right to be called 'moral', and which can be defined *formally* rather than in terms of *content*. These formal criteria may not be sufficient to give us everything we need, but they will at least serve to distinguish some kinds of moral thought and action from non-moral thought and action, without forcing us to assign a particular content to morality. The close analysis of moral language on which this account rests, and which is required to elucidate these criteria, has been done elsewhere, and I need not repeat it here at length.[2]

The criteria which a man's opinions must satisfy if they are to

---

[1] See, e.g. my *Logic and Sexual Morality* (Penguin), pp. 48–9.
[2] See R. M. Hare, *Freedom and Reason* (O.U.P.).

count as moral opinions are: (i) They must be impartial as between persons. (ii) They must be prescriptive. One might very roughly express these two criteria as follows: if someone expresses a moral opinion ('It is wrong to steal', 'It is a good thing to keep one's promises', or whatever), then (a) he is laying down a principle of behaviour, not just for one particular person or occasion, but for all people on all similar occasions;[1] (b) he commits himself to acting on that principle (though of course he may sometimes lack the means or the willpower so to act); that is, a moral opinion does not just make an *observation* about what is good or bad, but (if sincerely held) *prescribes* for the person, or commits him to, a certain type of behaviour. (iii) They must be overriding: that is, they must take precedence over his other opinions.

There are a number of questions which may be raised about this account, but the most important for our present argument is the notion of the impartiality of moral judgements ((i) above). The account suggests that, in making moral judgements, we consider other people as being on an equal footing with ourselves: what goes for us, goes for them too, and vice versa. Without this, it is suggested, the whole business of morality and inter-personal rules could not get started. Moreover, if a man's moral opinions have to *prescribe* conduct for others as well as for himself ((ii) above), the implication is that he regards them as equals: one might think that he could not advance these opinions with any show of reason, or with much chance of success, unless he so regarded them.

---

[1] For example, if somebody says that he did a certain thing because he would get a lot of money for it, this is probably not an impartial reason; for there is no indication that he would wish anybody else to do the same sort of thing to him. Thus if the act in question was that of defrauding somebody, he would not want somebody else to defraud him in this way. It might be a man's principle to get as much money for himself, always, as he could; but he would not prescribe such a principle impartially for everyone else.

Other people's interests
Now though the account itself defines moral judgements in purely
formal terms, the implication of the underlying notion of equality
suggests at least one obvious procedural principle for at least one
area that we usually call 'moral': perhaps the most important, or
the most typical, area. This is the area of interpersonal morality:
that is, the area where the wants and interests of individuals living
in society conflict, or may conflict. The procedural principle is
simply that the *sort of justification* needed for a moral view in
this area must relate to the feelings and interests of other people
(just as the sort of justification needed for a scientific view must
relate to observed empirical facts, experimental results, and so
forth). This is not to say *either* that moral or scientific views must
have a particular content – that we can dismiss certain specific
views as not moral, or not scientific – *or* that you can rationally
hold any moral view you like. It is simply to say that a moral
view, to count as rational, must be backed up by certain kinds of
reasons.

Of course people do hold views which might be called 'moral',
but which aren't necessarily backed up or justified in this rational
way. Imagine a man who thinks that the preservation of works of
art is more important than saving human life. This principle
might certainly be a moral principle, but whether it is sensible
depends on how he defends it. If he says (i) 'Well, future genera-
tions of men will gain pleasure and profit from these works of
art, so it's worth preserving them even if it costs human lives',
then it *might* be sensible because it's about other people's
interests: if he says (ii) 'Well, they are just so beautiful and mar-
vellous, even if no human beings existed they should be pre-
served', it looks very odd.

The significant point here is that when it comes to defending
views of this sort, a rational defence has to relate to human
interests. The second defence (ii) offered by the art-lover above
sounds implausible; we feel inclined to say, 'But what's the *point*
of keeping all these pictures if there are no human beings around
to enjoy them?', and hence more generally, 'What's the point of

anything apart from its relation to someone's interests and desires?' We allow people to use different criteria of justification when engaged in other activities (aesthetics, etiquette, science, mathematics, and so on); but this is partly because these activities as a whole either do serve human interests, or at least do not militate against them. But when it comes to overriding opinions, those which ultimately settle how a man behaves in relation to his fellows (even if he does not himself consider that relationship), we demand that these opinions be justified in the light of human interests. For when somebody holds up a rule of behaviour as something to be followed (by the use of words like 'good', 'ought', and 'right' that have a universal application), as opposed to merely expressing a selfish or personal desire or intention, then he thereby submits it to the judgement of all of us.

Of course there are some points here which can be disputed: and the reader who still feels inclined to dispute them can always read the relevant literature.[1] In partciular, he may still think three sorts of questions worth asking:

(1) Why bother about other people at all?

(2) Why bother about *all* other people? Couldn't we just confine our morality to *some* other people (only our family and friends, only our countrymen, only white people, only the over-21s, only the under-50s, etc.)?

(3) Why bother about their *interests*? Couldn't we have a reasonable morality which flowed from some picture or ideal which had nothing much to do with interests, but was conceived (say) in terms of 'honour', 'preserving the good name of the family', 'doing what God wanted', 'chivalry', 'acting like a gentleman', 'following one's deepest feelings', etc.?

There is no space here to go into these questions, though we shall try to say something about (3) in a later chapter (Chapter Five). In any case, I am not sure how far these are, for most of us in this society, really significant questions, though they may have an academic interest. I incline to think that there is an

---

[1] See *I.M.E.*, p. 102 *et seq.*, with footnotes and references.

important sense in which everybody really knows, once they think seriously about it, what morals are about: the difficulty is simply that people run wild and try to play other games instead. In the same way, it is of course *possible* to ask questions like, 'Why should we face facts?' or, 'Why shouldn't we contradict ourselves?' But it's not clear that such questions are *serious*, in one sense: they may be expressions of psychological dissatisfaction rather than genuine questions with proper answers.

'Being reasonable'

Some people may still feel worried at describing morals in terms of 'being reasonable'. But they need not. Words like 'rules', 'reasons', 'logical' and 'rational' on the one hand, and 'imagination', 'feeling', 'emotion' and 'commitment' on the other, may be used to present a false picture, a picture of mythical conflict of 'reason versus emotion' or 'faith versus logic'. Being rational or reasonable, however, does not mean disregarding one's feelings, but trying to assess, guide or direct them in some coherent way. If we make any sort of judgement at all about our feelings, commitments, etc. we cannot do so except by reference to some kind of standard, or rule, or principle: and words like 'right', 'justifiable', 'wise', 'sensible', 'authentic', 'unprejudiced', 'perceptive' and many others are tied to the notion of such standards. Hence, while it is correct to say that one's rules and standards must be one's own, and not accepted uncritically from authority, it is not correct to say that one can do without standards altogether – unless one wishes to resign one's humanity and live at random.

As far as I can see at present, I would say that abandoning these standards means resigning from being a person. One may say, 'Well, why be a person?'; but any answer to this would have to be given in terms which already imply the concept of a person. In so far as someone is still a person – particularly, in so far as he is prepared to *talk*, then rationality has a foothold, and we can do business. If he is not a person, then we can perhaps help to make him into one, as we do every day with newborn infants. If we make life such hell for him that he wants to resign from being a person, temporarily or permanently, then something has gone wrong and it is our fault. It is just because things so often go wrong in this way that philosophical description is not enough: we need not only to describe rationality, but to find out and produce the psychological and social factors that make rationality tolerable and, if possible, enjoyable.

four

What We Need for Morals

We should now be a bit clearer on the question of what morality is about: and it should thus not be too hard to make a list of the qualities which a person who was good at 'doing morals' would have. We could describe such a person as the 'morally educated' man: for, obviously, education should be able to help people acquire these qualities. Remember yet again that we are not saying that the 'morally educated' person will have this or that particular moral belief, or will act in this or that way; we are saying only that he will be reasonable or rational in his moral beliefs and actions.

A. A GENERAL ACCOUNT

We might start by trying to summarize some of the conclusions in the last chapter, which will give us some idea of the ways and senses in which a person's thought and action can be called 'reasonable' or 'rational' in morality:

(a) There is first the basic sense of 'rational', which we considered on pp. 33–34, the sense in which a person must act for a reason (rather than just as a result of outside causes). Someone who did not act for a reason would certainly not be acting in the *moral* sphere: indeed, he would not be *acting* (in the full sense) at all. (This also includes the case of the person who is rationalizing: i.e. who may say that he is acting for a reason, but in whom the reason is not actually operative.)

(b) In the sphere of interpersonal morality, where other people's interests are strongly affected, there is the person who acts for a reason, but whose reason has nothing to do with other people's interests and is therefore not appropriate. The thought and action of such a person would not be rational, because he is not following the rules of procedure relevant to this sphere of morality.

(c) There is the person who (in his moral thinking) is logically inconsistent, does not know all the relevant facts or refuses to face them, or does not sufficiently attend to the meanings of words. He is irrational in terms of those rules or principles which enter into other kinds of thinking as well as into morality.

(d) There is the person who does not use sufficient psychological awareness, perceptiveness or imagination, and who is hence no good at identifying his own and other people's feelings. He is irrational in terms of those principles which go beyond the principles in (c) above, and which are peculiarly essential to morality.

One very important point must now be noted. The above list is not *simply* a list of skills, abilities or competences. In (c), for instance, we talked of the man who 'does not know all the relevant facts or refuses to face them', and these are two very different things. Similarly the man in (d) who 'does not use sufficient psychological awareness' may *either* not have the skill or ability to know what other people are feeling, *or* he may *have* the ability but *just not use it*. In other words, we have not distinguished in this list between (i) a person being morally educated in the sense of having the relevant skills and abilities, and (ii) a person being morally educated in the sense of actually using these skills and abilities in his moral life.

The latter connects with what we said earlier (pp. 36–37) about *people* being reasonable or unreasonable. We have to recognize that a man may be quite reasonable, and yet be unable to use the relevant skills and abilities (perhaps simply because he has not been taught them); and conversely, that a man may be possessed of all the skills and abilities, and yet himself be unreasonable (and hence not in fact use them). We are all familiar with people who have at least some of these skills – who are highly intelligent, know a great many facts, are good at logic, and so on – and yet rarely bring them to bear when they actually make their moral decisions. Their emotions get in the way, or they are lazy, or in one way or another *they* are unreasonable in their moral living: even though they may be extremely rational in other areas (they may be very good scientists or politicians, for instance). Equally we are familiar with people who are extremely reasonable – they are open-minded, anxious to learn, unmoved by misplaced fears or impulses, and so on – but who yet cannot reach reasonable moral beliefs simply because they are uninstructed. Neither type of person is fully educated in the moral sphere.

The notion of *people* being reasonable or unreasonable comes into the matter in yet another way. We may regard the list above as characterizing the person who not only has certain skills, but actually uses them in making his moral decisions. But there is still a gap between decision and action. A person may be wholly rational in making up his mind what he ought to do: he may be logical, perceptive, know all the facts, etc., and he may actually use all these abilities when presented with a moral problem: but he may still *act* irrationally. There may be a fatal disjunction between his thought and his behaviour. Inappropriate emotions may intervene, not before or during his moral thinking, but before or during his actions: he suddenly becomes afraid, or yields to impulse, or grows apathetic. We need therefore to add to our list by mentioning:

(e) The person who has and uses all these skills, but fails to translate them into action because he is himself unreasonable in this respect.[1]

---

[1] We normally list such cases under two headings: (*a*) those who are blameworthy, and could have acted rightly if only they had tried; (*b*) those who are not to be blamed because they couldn't help it. 'Unreasonable' can apply to cases of both types: not only to those who are weak-willed, but also to the neurotic and other 'mental health' cases. The well-known problems about blame and free will are of course connected with our general thesis, but I don't think we need wait on their solution; they are not the *same* problems as problems about what is meant by calling people 'unreasonable'. See Professor Strawson's *Freedom and Resentment* (O.U.P.).

B. 'CONSCIENCE' AND 'MORAL AUTHORITIES'

These considerations may help to evaluate the very popular notion of 'acting according to one's conscience', which may be briefly mentioned here. The notion of conscience is a compound of two logically distinct elements, (i) what one might describe as a 'raw' *feeling* of guilt, fear, taboo or whatever, and (ii) some kind of propositional *belief* or judgement about what is right.[1] Now if we ask the general question, 'Should one act according to one's conscience?', this may mean (i) 'Should we follow our "raw" feelings of guilt, etc?': and the answer to this is obvious, namely, 'Sometimes we should and sometimes we shouldn't'. Alternatively, it may mean (ii) 'Should we do what we believe or judge to be right?', to which the answer is equally obvious, namely, 'Yes, of course, what else can we reasonably do (even though we may sometimes judge mistakenly)?'

It is also perhaps worth while trying to spell out the relevant points about the notion of a 'moral authority' somewhat more clearly. They amount to the following:

1. Somebody may have 'moral authority' in that sense of 'moral' which really means having some kind of psychological hold or power over others. When people appear to be giving reasons for their moral actions, such as, 'I felt compelled to follow him', or, 'He impressed me so much with his presence that I felt I ought to do what he said', or, 'I was driven by the power of Jesus/the magnetism of Hitler/the deep sincerity of Gandhi to do so-and-so', they may well be admitting to a compulsion rather than quoting a reason.

2. People may also pose as 'moral authorities' in another sense, i.e. as people who by some method 'know the right answer' to moral problems. Whether they can be accepted as real authorities depends, not on whether they happen to get what we later come to regard as the right answer, and certainly not on whether they make some kind of psychological appeal to us, but simply on whether they have shown themselves better than other men at

---

[1] See pp. 32–33.

using the skills, and hence at fulfilling the criteria of rationality, which are appropriate to morality.

3. It is probable that various people will be, in this sense, authorities in *different* aspects of morality. Thus, some will be good at attending to the hard facts, others at the meaning of words, others at knowing what people feel, and so forth. It would thus be rash to accept anyone as a moral authority without qualification; the temptation to do so would derive from the idea, that moral knowledge depends on some single quality of intuition or perception.

4. To be a moral authority is not to be good at communicating or teaching morality, for which other skills and talents are also involved, in the same way as to be a good historian is not necessarily to be a good teacher of history.

5. It may be reasonable to accept the word of a moral authority, but the choice to accept a moral authority is still our own choice, and the reasonableness of accepting the authority's word depends on the reasonableness of accepting the person as an authority in the first place.

6. Even where it is reasonable to do this, there are still good arguments for preferring that, as far as possible, people should themselves directly perceive the appropriate reasons for their moral views at first-hand.

Possible arguments here are:

(a) because this will result in a more secure psychological basis for their morality, a basis which they have appropriated for themselves and by their own efforts;

(b) because part of the point of morality is to adopt the right attitude towards other people within oneself, not merely to do the right thing.

7. Hence we should do best to regard moral authorities as primarily useful in the following ways:

(a) as people whose skills we can attempt to emulate;

(b) as people whose precepts may help us to do the right thing (even if we do not ourselves see why it is right), which will at

the very least keep us from actively disturbing the interests of
other people;

(c) as people whose precepts may give us a framework of action,
which we can use to develop the right attitudes which are
central to morality.

C. THE MORAL COMPONENTS

We are now in a position to list the skills, abilities, etc. that the
morally educated person will need. It is best not to do this in
terms of such words as 'unselfishness', 'altruism', 'determination',
'awareness', 'sensitivity', and so forth, for it is often not at all
clear just what these words mean. Here I shall follow a convention used in another book,[1] and list components under the
heading of some monosyllabic technical terms (borrowed from
Greek) – PHIL, EMP, GIG and so forth. In each case we shall
first describe the component, say something about the different
ways in which it may operate, and put down a few questions
which one might want to ask in order to see whether a person
had that particular component or not.

PHIL

A. WHAT IS PHIL?

PHIL is an *attitude* or a frame of mind: it is not simply an ability
or a piece of knowledge. Various ways of describing this attitude
might be 'regarding other people as equals', 'thinking that other
people's interests count', 'weighing other people's interests equally
with one's own', 'looking on other people as human beings with
rights', 'taking notice of other people's wants and needs', 'not
thinking that one's own interests are a special case', 'having a
concern for their interests', 'caring about others', and so on.

1. Attitudes like PHIL are detected and verified by the way in
which a person thinks in his everyday, practical living, and to
some extent by the way in which he acts. We must be careful

---

[1] *I.M.E.*, p. 192 *et seq.*

here, however, because it is possible for a person to have this attitude but not to act on it – perhaps because he does not know how to, or because he is frightened, or for some other reason: and failures of this kind would be failures of KRAT, not of PHIL.[1] However, the person must to *some* extent act up to his attitude: in the extreme case, if he never did so, we should rightly doubt whether he sincerely had that attitude. In this respect PHIL differs from EMP and GIG:[2] EMP and GIG are respectively an ability and an attainment, and a person may have these without ever actually using them in his everyday life. PHIL, on the other hand, must to some extent be detectable in a person's practical living.

2. On the cognitive side, PHIL involves a *belief* – the belief that other people have equal rights with oneself. (This relates to 1. above: if beliefs are genuine, they to some extent show themselves in action.) This belief should normally go along with an emotion or *feeling* – that of respect for other people – and the two merge into an attitude adopted towards them. We have to beware, however, of misinterpreting PHIL in two ways:

(a) By regarding it as *only* a matter of belief: i.e. as long as the person says he believes in the equality of other people's interests, that is sufficient. The danger of this can be shown by considering the example of a person who says (and perhaps in some sense really thinks) that he is not prejudiced against Negroes and regards them as equals, but who in his feelings and behaviour shows quite clearly that he is.

(b) By regarding some intense feeling (e.g. of brotherhood, love, strong sympathy, etc.) as necessary for PHIL. This is not in fact necessary. The degree to which strong feelings of this kind are desirable is questionable, and in any case is (at least for our present purposes) more a matter of mental health than morals. The person with PHIL must feel sufficiently to act on his belief in equality, but need not feel more. Thus it is

---

[1] See below under KRAT.
[2] See below under EMP and GIG.

sufficient if an older boy thinks that a nervous new boy needs some help (rather than dismissing him because he is a new boy, stupid, too young to bother about, etc.) and actually helps him; it is not required that the older boy himself goes through (or has earlier gone through) parallel agonies of nervousness.

3. It is important to realize what is meant by 'other *people*'. It is not in virtue of their having two legs or one head that we think human beings to have rights and to be equals. Rather it is because they have desires, wants, feelings, and purposes; they are conscious and (to a greater or lesser degree) intelligent and rational. (A religious person might put this by saying that they have souls.) This distinguishes human beings from the lower animals, plants, and physical objects. The importance of this point is that many people, consciously or unconsciously, seem to assume that some other criterion is what really counts – e.g. whether they have white skins, or talk English, or come from a similar social class, or are members of the same gang. Our criterion would enable us to include (if and when necessary!) all 'people', even if from another planet and with tentacles instead of arms.[1]

4. Similarly it should be clear what is meant by regarding other people as *equals*. We do not of course mean that a person should consider other people to be equally clever, heavy, rich, etc. as himself: they may be more or less so. We mean rather that he should give them equality of status as conscious beings, each of whose wills and desires count as much as his own. It is in this sense that 'all men are equal' points to an important truth.[2]

5. It is not required that a person should consider another person as *more* important than himself: only as of *equal* importance. He should not be afraid to stand up for his rights, or to make his own wants and interests felt. Of course it is possible that

[1] On this point C. S. Lewis's *Out of the Silent Planet* is illuminating.
[2] See John Wilson, *Equality* (Hutchinson, 1966).

he may *prefer* to abandon his own immediate interests for the sake of another, indeed in so far as a person can genuinely feel unselfish and love it is to be expected that this will happen. But we should beware of pseudo-unselfishness and pseudo-altruism here. Genuine altruism involves a further stage of moral education which goes beyond justice and equality: it is not entailed by what we mean here by PHIL.

B. DIMENSIONS IN PHIL

6. We may distinguish two important dimensions in PHIL:

(a) *Scope*. This is, roughly, *how many* other people a person is prepared to include in his attitude of respect or equality. Thus some will show PHIL only for people of the same age-group, in the same gang, of the same race, etc.; others will extend it more widely.

(b) *Amount*. This is *not* (see 2 (b) above) the intensity of feeling which a person has, but roughly how often or how consistently a person shows PHIL within whatever range his PHIL operates. Thus if a person shows PHIL towards (say) members of the same gang, there is still a question about how often he does so: his PHIL may operate 100 per cent of the time within this range, or at a lower degree.

C. QUESTIONS FOR PHIL

Does the person even *say* that all other human beings have rights of equal importance with his own? Or does he consciously believe that coloured people, Jews, those of a different social class, etc. really are 'inferior'?

If he says he believes in equality, is he *just* saying it, or does he really *mean* it? Is he just paying lip-service to a fashionable way of thinking, or does he really believe it?

If he does believe it, does he show forth this belief in his behaviour? Does he really *adopt* the attitude of PHIL?

How does he actually *treat* certain people (whom perhaps he might look down on, or be unreasonably in awe of): e.g. nervous new boys, pupils of the opposite sex, authority-figures, coloured people, etc.). Does he treat them as equals or not?

Does he listen to their opinions and allow them to have their say? If he and his group are deciding what to do, does he allow what *they* want to count? Or does he dismiss what they want as unimportant?

If a quite different kind of person from those he is used to comes within his experience – a foreigner, for instance, or somebody whose social behaviour is very unlike his own – does he regard him as an 'outsider', or does he accept him as equal with himself even though his behaviour is different?

Does he make some *effort* to find out what other people's wants and feelings actually are, however good or bad his ability to discern this (EMP) may be?

EMP

A. WHAT IS EMP?

EMP is an *ability,* not a feeling or an attitude. Concern for other people – the general feeling or attitude that their interests count – is PHIL; EMP is simply the ability to know what oneself and other people are feeling, or would feel, or have felt, in particular situations. Rough definitions might be 'awareness' of one's own and other people's feelings', 'insight', 'the ability to understand what people's interests are', 'knowledge of human emotions, desires, etc.', (EMP is thus *coextensive* with PHIL). EMP must not be confused with *sympathy*, which is not an ability but a feeling.

1. The ability of EMP is thus something which may, at least in principle, be disjoined from PHIL. It is possible for someone to know what others are feeling, or would be likely to feel, with a very high degree of awareness or insight, and yet not to *care* about them. (A dictator who was very good at manipulating other people's emotions for his own selfish ends would be an example.)

2. Since EMP is an ability and not a behavioural trait, it is possible for a person to have a high degree of EMP and yet not

actually to *use* this ability very much in practice. For instance, he may be very nervous about people, and hence too frightened to observe them closely in everyday life: or he may be lazy, and not bother: nevertheless he may still have the ability to tell what other people are feeling, and if only he was not nervous or lazy he would use it. (Of course if he *is* and always has been nervous or lazy about other people, he will probably not in fact have developed very much EMP: but the distinction is still an important one.)

3. EMP is concerned not only with awareness of the feelings of people with whom one actually comes into contact in one's everyday life: it includes also being able to predict the feelings of those whom one has never met – people in other countries, in the future, in the past, and so on – and one's own feelings, which is often the most difficult of all.

4. By 'feelings' we are not primarily concerned with sensations but with emotions and desires. These can be detected in human beings in the following ways:

(i) By what a person *says* he feels: e.g. 'I'm frightened'.
(ii) By characteristic *symptoms*: e.g. trembling at the knees, sweating, etc.
(iii) By characteristic *action*: e.g. running away from the danger.
(iv) By characteristic *circumstances*: e.g. dangerous things.

The person with a high degree of EMP will know about all these, in the case of all the human emotions, and also be able to correlate them. Thus he will know that stammering and turning pale are characteristic symptoms or nervousness or anxiety: he will also know what the person with these symptoms is likely to say and do, and he will have some idea about what circumstances are making him nervous. All these are ideally required if someone is to have full and proper knowledge of another person's feelings.

B. DIMENSIONS IN EMP

5. These are much the same as for PHIL. To repeat them briefly:

(a) *Scope* – how many of other people's feelings he has the ability to be aware of.
(b) *Degree* – how precise and profound his awareness of those feelings is.

c. QUESTIONS FOR EMP

Can the person give a reasonably good account of the feelings of (say) a new boy at the school, or his own teacher, or his classmates in particular situations?

Does he find it difficult or easy to understand why, in school and outside it, different people behave as they do?

Does he find this difficult or easy with reference to people in past history?

With reference to characters in plays or novels?

Can he act or play the role of other people effectively (someone being bullied, a foreigner arriving in a strange country, a criminal, etc.)?

Has he a fair idea of what is meant by the words which stand for people's feelings ('jealousy', 'anxiety', 'aggression', 'love', etc.)?

Has he the ability to detect and be honest about *his own* feelings?

Has he the courage and emotional maturity to discuss his own feelings, whether or not he has the necessary vocabulary, skill in discussion, etc. to do so?

Whatever his ability, is he *interested* in his own and other people's feelings and behaviour, or are his ideas about them based on no observation and thinking at all?

Is he competent at identifying and correlating what he and other people say they feel, their symptoms, their behaviour, and the surrounding circumstances (see 4. above)?

GIG (1)

A. WHAT IS GIG (1)?

GIG (1) is perhaps the most easily describable of the components. It is an *attainment*: that is, we are here concerned with whether a person *actually knows* certain facts (not with whether he has the ability to learn them): namely, those facts most relevant to moral situations.

1. The kind of facts relevant to GIG (1) are 'hard' facts: not facts about people's feelings and desires, which come under EMP.

2. Plainly almost any such facts *might* be relevant to moral decisions: moreover, people in particular jobs or situations (e.g. doctors or lawyers) would be expected to know a great many more facts of a certain kind than other people would be expected to know. However, for practical purposes GIG (1) may be divided into two areas:

(i) Knowledge of the laws, rules and contracts of a person's society, and of the social system in general: also knowledge of conventions and social expectations.

(ii) Knowledge of what things are dangerous to human beings in that society and elsewhere, including knowledge of relevant facts about the human body.

(These are repeated more fully below.)

3. In considering a person's GIG (1), we must (regrettably) resist the temptation to make allowance for his I.Q., home background, and so forth. We are simply interested in how many of the relevant facts a person knows. Whether or not it is his *fault*, if he knows very few facts, does not matter. Neither with GIG, nor with any of the other components, are we interested in assigning any particular kind of moral *blame* or guilt, only in establishing how far that person is morally educated.

B. QUESTIONS FOR GIG (1)

Does he have a resonable knowledge of:

(i) The laws and rules enforced in his country and his local community (including the school), at least of those likely to affect him: and about the conventions and social expectations of his own and other social groups – what sort of manners are acceptable, what words and ritual phrases to use, how people react to certain kinds of dress, language, behaviour, etc.?

The general working of the society in which he finds himself? The implicit or explicit contracts which operate in members of that society?

(ii) What is dangerous and not dangerous to standard interests of other people – e.g. putting things on railway lines, excessively fast driving, effects of certain drugs, etc.; also relevant facts in human biology and physiology – e.g. first aid, facts about pregnancy and other sexual matters, etc.?

GIG (2)

A. WHAT IS GIG (2)?

A person may possess and use the components so far listed – PHIL, EMP, GIG (1) – and yet fail to translate his moral decision into effective action. One reason for this may be that he lacks sufficient motivation, resolution or courage; this we shall consider under KRAT, our final component. But another reason may be that he lacks what we might call the 'know-how'. He might decide, for instance, to try to be nice to a new boy in a school and cheer him up; and he may be adequately motivated or resolved to put his decision into action; but he may not know *how to* be nice and cheer him up – perhaps he does not know just what words to use, or cannot speak to him without sounding patronizing, and so forth. The general abilities required for effective action of this kind we shall call 'social skills' (GIG (2)).

1. It must be recognized that 'social skills' are not confined to group-situations, where (for instance) we might expect a person to be able to make the right sort of remarks at a party: they include abilities which are required for person-to-person behaviour as well. In this sense one might fail, e.g. to treat one's wife properly for lack of the relevant 'social skill'.

2. Social skills are of course closely connected in practice with EMP (knowledge of his own and other people's feelings) and GIG (1) (knowledge of facts, including facts about social norms and conventions). But the ability to act effectively towards other people demands more than this. The *kind* of knowledge is

different: it is more like knowing how to swim, or how to play a
particular game -- not just a matter of knowing facts, but also
a matter of being sufficiently practised and skilful to *perform*
well. It is a kind of adeptness rather than a cognitive mastery of
facts.

3. There are many different areas of social skills, depending
on the context in which they are exercised. Thus the ability to
discuss among equals is one thing: the ability to give orders is
another: to take orders, yet another: and so on. We are chiefly
interested here in those contexts and social relationships in which
it is likely that most people will be called upon to perform: e.g.
with groups of friends, as an employee, as a member of a committee, and so on.

B. QUESTIONS FOR GIG (2)
Is he capable of playing the rôle of leader, of issuing instructions
    and orders?
Can he behave efficiently in social situations involving (a) adults,
    (b) people much younger than himself?
Can he behave well in formal or conventional contexts, and in
    less formal contexts?
Can he discuss the debate effectively with his equals?
Can he co-operate in decision-making, e.g. on a committee?
Does he put other people at their ease in social situations?
Does he in general use language adequately in social situations?

DIK

A. WHAT IS DIK?
DIK is best described as a *stage* or as a *mode of thought*. A person
with a high degree of DIK, when he faces up to a moral situation
(various kinds of failure to face up to such situations may be
caused by lack of KRAT),[1] will consider that situation primarily

---

[1] See below, pp. 62–64.

in terms of other people's interests. He will bring the appropriate attitude (PHIL), his ability to discern other people's feelings (EMP), and his knowledge of 'hard' facts (GIG (1)), to bear on that situation: and as a result he will make a prescriptive moral choice, dictated by other people's interests, which he regards as committing him and anyone else in a similar situation to *action*. Such a person will normally have a number of *moral principles*, which he has arrived at in this way.

1. It is not required, of course, that a person should go through this procedure every time he is faced with a moral situation. A reasonable person should already have formulated at least some moral principles or generalizations, and have the settled habit of acting on them without too much thought. But a person with DIK would be able, if asked, to give at least some indication of *why* he behaved as he did – however habitual or unplanned his action was; and his reasons would relate to other people's interests. *Mere* habit is not enough: it has to be habit generated by an earlier process of moral reasoning, of the kind described.

2. We have to remember[1] that the notion of 'having a moral principle' or 'making a moral choice' carries with it the notion that a person who makes such a choice does not make it for himself alone or for that situation only. Moral choices are of the form 'I – and anyone else in the same position – ought to do so-and-so': or to put it another way, of the form 'one ought', not just 'I' or 'you' or 'he ought'. This is important, because morality is a matter of prescribing what is right for human beings in general to do. We must also remember that moral choices are *overriding*. That is, the person who says, 'I ought to do so-and-so' has to mean more than just that he thinks it right, in a mild way, that he should do it – with the implication that, if things become difficult or he is going to suffer for it, then it would no longer be the right thing to do. He has got to think that it is *the* right thing for *him* to *do* in that situation, not just something which it would be nice to do in principle.

----

[1] See earlier, pp. 39–40.

B. DIMENSIONS OF DIK

DIK is a complex moral component, but the two most important dimensions may be described briefly as follows:

(a) *Right reasons*. Not everybody makes, or even thinks he ought to make, his moral decisions on the basis of other people's interests. Other modes of thought besides DIK are regrettably common. Amongst these are: obedience to authority, conformity to what one's social group thinks or expects, guilt-feelings, non-rational obedience to rules, a tendency to do what is most expedient for oneself, following one's immediate impulses, and just having a vague and unrationalized feeling that something is right or wrong. Nearly everybody uses some one or other non-DIK mode of thought in *some* area of moral choice (sexual behaviour is a good example). The person with a high degree of DIK will always consider other people's interests, and think in this mode rather than in others.

(b) *Sincerity of decision*. There are also people who may pay lip-service to a certain mode of moral thinking (whether DIK or some other), and say that certain things would be right or wrong, but who do not sincerely *commit* themselves in making these judgements. They may call something 'good' or say that one 'ought' to do it, but they may not use these words in a way which really *prescribes action on their part*. (For instance, they may just mean by 'good', 'what is commonly supposed to be good'.) The person with DIK will not just evaluate moral situations by reference to other people's interests, but actually make his moral *choices* and decisions, and commit himself by reference to those interests.

C. QUESTIONS FOR DIK

Does he think that morals are 'just a matter of taste', 'all relative', etc., or does he believe that there are right and wrong answers to moral questions?

Does he think that other people's interests are what *ought* to count in a moral situation, or does he think that moral questions should be settled by other means (obeying an authority, avoiding a sense of guilt or shame, doing what everybody else does, doing what pays, etc.)?

If he does believe in taking other people's interests into account, does he actually do this in his moral thinking, or does he in fact follow some other criterion (what authority tells him, sense of guilt, etc.)?

Does he make use of whatever PHIL, EMP and GIG he has for his moral decisions?

When he uses words like 'good', 'bad', 'right', 'wrong', 'ought', etc., does he use them in such a way as really to commit himself to acting in a certain way, or does he just mean what other people (perhaps just adults) *think* is good (. . . . right, etc.): i.e. to what extent does he really have a *prescriptive* moral vocabulary at all?

When he makes moral judgements, does he really believe that they apply to *all* people in similar situations, including himself (universalisability)?

Does he have a reasonably coherent set of moral principles – not necessarily completely fixed and certain, but at any rate seriously held for obvious cases (murder, stealing, lying, etc.)?

Do his principles include not only avoiding bad actions, but doing good ones (not only not harming other people, but actively and positively helping them)?

KRAT

A. WHAT IS KRAT?

The five previous components – PHIL, EMP, GIG (1) and (2), and DIK – are all components of moral *thinking*: an attitude, an ability, an attainment, a mode of thought and other abilities. KRAT is quite different. Here we are concerned with *action* or *behaviour*. Anything that is required over and above the other components for rational moral action and behaviour will come under the head of KRAT. Something like 'behavioural traits necessary for morality' might serve as a partial definition; however it is plain enough that KRAT does not stand for any one thing, but rather for an assortment of things any or all of which may be required for appropriate moral behaviour.

1. KRAT-traits enter into a person's moral thought and action in two basic ways.

(a) A person must have the alertness and sensitivity actually to *use* the other components in his moral thinking, as opposed to having the abilities, etc. but not actually using them:

(b) When a person has reached a rational moral decision, he must have the motivation and resolution to translate that decision into action.

2. It is a mistake to think of KRAT simply in terms of will-power. There are all sorts of reasons why people fail to bring their abilities to bear on moral situations, or fail to translate their moral decisions into action. They may be forgetful, incompetent, lazy, frightened, tired, cowardly, etc., and not all of these are what would normally be called *moral* failures.

3. The complexities of KRAT are very considerable, and the best we can do here is to list some generalized KRAT-traits that seem of particular importance:

(i) A person should have a sufficient *sentiment* or love for other people; this is at least *one* kind of motivation which should enable him both to think and act rationally in the moral sphere.

(ii) A person should have 'good habits', or a settled disposition to think and act in a rational manner, irrespective of his feelings at the time. One cannot perhaps feel sentiment towards other people all the time, and this kind of motivation seems of very great practical importance.

(iii) A person must possess independence of judgement, the ability to think and act autonomously (as opposed simply to following other people like a sheep), and sufficient courage to act on his judgement; this seems a necessary quality, since there will be plenty of cases where rational morality goes against what is publicly acceptable.

(iv) A person must be reflective or thoughtful enough not to be carried away by particular situations, and not to be forgetful of other people. He needs fixed habits, but he also must be able to stop and think when required. He needs, as it were, some kind of warning system which operates in him and tells him to think about what he is doing before he does anything.

B. QUESTIONS FOR KRAT

Does he *feel* strongly and favourably enough towards other people for him to be adequately motivated in thinking morally and in actually carrying out his moral principles?

Does he have good and settled habits which enable him to translate his moral principles into action without difficulty?

Does he have sufficient independence of judgement or 'conscience' to make up his own mind and act in moral situations, regardless of what other people think?

Does he have sufficient sensitivity for situations involving other people to stop and think before acting?

Here are two examples of how these components would work in practice:

1. A six-former, has enough PHIL to care for new boys who have just arrived at the school. He knows that Bloggs is a new boy (GIG (1)), and perceives that Bloggs is nervous, feeling a bit left out of things, etc. (EMP). He is sufficiently motivated and able to face this general situation, and to bring his PHIL, GIG (1) and EMP to bear (KRAT). Consequently, he decides to do the right thing – DIK – i.e. to try to make the new boy feel at home. He keeps this decision steadily in mind, isn't frightened of carrying it out for fear of being laughed at, isn't distracted from it by his own desires, etc. (KRAT). He has the awareness (EMP), the factual knowledge (GIG (1)), and the 'know-how' or 'social skill' (GIG (2)) to carry out his decision effectively – i.e. to talk to the boy in the right sort of way, ask him to join in the games, or whatever would in fact help to make him feel at home. Having all these, he acts rightly.

2. A car driver, has enough PHIL to care for other car drivers,

SUMMARY

List of Components

NAME	STATUS	ROUGH DEFINITION	DETAILS
PHIL	Attitude	regarding others as equals, taking their interests as equally important.	(i) scope (how many 'others') (ii) degree (how firm/consistent the attitude)
EMP	Ability	ability to know what oneself and others are feeling, and what their interests are.	(i) scope (how many 'others') (ii) degree (amount and precision of knowledge)
GIG (1)	Attainment	knowledge of 'hard' facts relevant to moral choices.	(i) law, contracts, and social norms (ii) danger, safety, human biology. etc.
GIG (2)	Ability	practical 'know-how' to perform effectively in social contexts.	
DIK	Mode of thought	ability to prescribe action for oneself for right reasons.	(i) rightness of reasons (ii) sincerity of decision
KRAT	Motivation and behavioural traits	factors required (a) to use the other components, (b) to translate consequent moral judgement into action.	(i) alertness (ii) resolution

to count their suffering or inconvenience as important. He sees
that another driver is trying to turn from a side road into a very
heavy stream of traffic on the main road, and knows that it will
be difficult for him (GIG (1)). He knows – having himself been
in the same situation – how maddening and worrying it is to be
in this position (EMP). He has enough KRAT to connect his PHIL,
GIG (1) and EMP together: so he decides that the right thing
to do is to stop for a few seconds and let the other driver join the
main traffic (DIK). He has enough KRAT not·to be worried by
the stupid hooting of the main-stream drivers behind him, and
enough GIG (1) to realize that it will not cause any significant
delay to the main-stream. He also has the 'know-how' (GIG (2))
to be able to let him into the main stream in a nice way, e.g.
stopping and waving him in with a friendly smile, not in an
officious and bad-tempered manner.

You may easily think up such examples yourself, or analyse
actual moral situations in this way. It may be helpful finally to
formalize these in terms of two equations, as follows:
(1) PHIL EMP GIG (1), together with KRAT, leads to DIK (right
    decision);
(2) DIK, together with continued KRAT, plus further use of
    EMP, GIG (1) and GIG (2), leads to right action.

These skills, abilities and attitudes, then, are what you need
for making reasonable decisions about what to do, and for carrying out those decisions effectively. You may at this point want to
know how, in practice, a person can develop these moral components. How can a person learn to treat others as equals (PHIL),
or to be aware of his own and other people's feelings (EMP)?
How can he learn to acquire the alertness, resolution, and motivation necessary for using these and other abilities, and for trans-
lating them into action (KRAT)? Learning the 'hard facts'
(GIG (1)) and practising the 'social skills' (GIG (2)) may seem com-
paratively easy: but the other components may appear to be
unteachable.

In a narrow sense of the word, they may be for the most part
'unteachable': that is, the best ways of educating people in these

components may not take the form of classroom periods. Obviously the development of them is very much bound up with psychological and social factors – a person's home background, his early childhood, the kind of family and friends he has, how intelligent he is, what sort of teachers teach him, and many others. But it is also likely that some kind of 'direct method' teaching of the moral components will be effective.

Research is being done on what sorts of things can be done, in schools and elsewhere, to develop the components effectively. At present we can only guess. Below I have listed some guesses which might be useful for schools and colleges:

(1) Making sure that the concept of moral education is properly understood.

(2) Making whatever basic arrangements are necessary to bring the pupils into close communication with the staff.

(3) Making sure that the 'ground rules' of the institution are (a) based on the right *sort* of criteria (even if there is uncertainty about the facts), and (b) firmly enforced.

(4) Making the rules, and the point of the rules, as clear as possible to the pupils.

(5) Giving the pupils some degree of self-government, and establishing close communication in rule-making and rule-following.

(6) Decentralizing the institution to produce psychologically viable groups (e.g. a house system): basing the groups on factors that genuinely unite (e.g., perhaps, eating together, entertaining other groups, and other group activities which are significant to the children), without producing an artificial or illiberal community.

(7) Providing outlets for aggression, both in the 'letting off steam' sense (e.g. enough violent open-air activities) and in the 'challenging authority' sense (e.g. matches against the staff), that are unsophisticated enough to fit even the most primitive pupils (some kind of controlled fighting game, snow-balling, battles in the swimming bath, etc.).

(8) Providing contexts which will significantly occupy the institution as a whole (e.g. some construction enterprise, mass camping or exploring, dancing, singing, etc.).

(9) Arranging the criteria of success in the institution, in so far as some competition is inevitable (and perhaps desirable), so that everyone succeeds in something and acquires some prestige and self-confidence thereby.

(10) Arranging that there is some one person (e.g. the headmaster who acts as the ultimate authority (at least in a psychological sense, so far as the pupils are concerned); and who is actually on the premises, and visibly concerned with the day-to-day running of the school or college.

(11) Making the significant teaching unit a small group, with the same 'teacher' or adult group-leader, perhaps over a period of years, with whom the pupils can form a close personal relationship: and fitting 'specialist' or subject-teaching as far as possible into this framework.

(12) Making more use of older pupils to supervise and help the younger.

(13) Understanding of concepts and meaning: this (in an elementary form) involves the notion of 'philosophy' and is designed to produce awareness and mastery of different language uses.

(14) Understanding the general concepts, and the basic facts, of psychology and the social sciences, perhaps particularly anthropology.

(15) Mastery of other facts relevant to the prevailing morality of the pupil's society: e.g. the law, the system of government, the economic system, the 'professional ethics' attaching to certain jobs, etc.

(16) The use of other subjects, perhaps particularly history and literature, designed to increase awareness of other people in society, to reinforce and correlate with (14) and (15) above.

(17) Activities designed to objectify moral or psychological problems: e.g. mime, drama, 'acting out' various rôles (the

bully, the cheat, the practical joker, and so forth), controlled 'group therapy' sessions in which family and other problems are discussed overtly, discussions of particular case-histories of other people (taken from books, films or elsewhere).

(18) Using 'psychological documentary' films and tape-recordings, with subsequent discussion to objectify the pupil's own problems.

(19) Teaching the pupil to talk clearly, describe, dispute and acquire other language-using skills.

(20) Using music and the arts, as relevant to the way in which emotions are objectified.

(21) 'Religious education' used as a method of obtaining insight and a sane outlook on life as a whole.

(22) Various kinds of games, designed to clarify the concept of rule-following, the point, purpose and mutability of rules, the notion of *contracting for* certain rules, etc.

(23) The use of 'games', in the sense of microcosmic controlled situations, acted out for special purposes under specific rules (e.g. the pupils act out a 'democracy', a 'dictatorship', etc.); the teaching of particular concepts by means of these games (equality, honesty, duty, justice and so on).

(24) Teaching related to practical living, e.g. on sex, marriage, infant care, driving cars, dress and cosmetics, the use of money, etc.[1]

---

[1] The point of this would not be purely to make the content of education more 'real' or 'practical'. It is rather that signs of mental health or ill-health can be clearly pointed out in these areas. For instance, the purpose of teaching children about the use of money would not be solely or even chiefly to explain how little a pound will buy these days, or how you can get a mortgage: one would also want to show how and why people have very different attitudes to money, and how these are more or less rational. Similarly with dress, driving cars, sex and so forth. Thus it isn't so much that people don't know how to drive, in any simple sense: it's just that they sometimes drive, as we say, *like lunatics*. And 'sex education' isn't just a matter of telling the children *facts* (nor of laying down moral codes either); it's a matter of improving their awareness and self-control.

(25) Opportunities to 'patronize' and feel needed, i.e. to be responsible for and of service to younger children, old people, the poor, the lonely, animals, etc.

(26) Use of practical 'order-and-command' contexts, to see the point of discipline relevant to particular situations (e.g. in sailing, mountaineering, building and other operations with highly specific goals).

But these *are* only guesses. Some of them may be no good at all; and certainly there will be other things which are not mentioned here, but which may well be far more effective. Students, whether in sixth forms or colleges, are just as likely to be able to think of effective methods as anyone else, so if you use your imagination, you may be able to produce some very useful new ideas – and perhaps get them tried out in the school or college. You need to have a firm grasp of the moral components to start with, and you'll probably need to spend a bit of time re-reading the description of them given earlier in this chapter. But it's well worth while thinking and trying to do something about it, because the whole business of morality is obviously very important: just as important, I think, as most of the things one learns in schools and college – and often more interesting.

D. SOME COMMON MISTAKES

Meanwhile, it may be helpful to end by saying something about what the 'morally educated' person would look like; or perhaps, it would be better to say something about what such a person would *not* look like. We have already said that such a person would have the moral components – PHIL, EMP, GIG, DIK and KRAT – in a fully-developed form, but what sorts of ways are there in which people seem to avoid having or using these components? What sort of life-styles are marks of a person who is *not* morally educated?

It would obviously be wrong to say, for instance, 'The morally educated person would vote Labour, not have sexual experience before marriage, disapprove of the war in Vietnam', etc. For as we have stressed throughout, moral education is emphatically *not* a matter of persuading people to behave in certain ways laid down by other people: it is a matter of helping the individual to decide and act more reasonably for himself. Nevertheless, such an individual would, I think, have certain very general distinguishing marks. It may be useful to mention some of these so that, in practice, we can check up on ourselves and avoid some of the more obvious pitfalls.

1. *'Charity begins at home'*

It is characteristic of many human beings that they cannot solve (or even face) their immediate problems, but carry these unsolved problems over into some other part of their lives, often with disastrous effects. The child who felt himself unloved, the unattractive adolescent who couldn't keep a steady job, grows up to take his revenge on the world as Adolf Hitler. The boy who felt that he could never really get through to his mother grows up into the compulsive Casanova who seduces girl after girl, in a vain attempt to make up for what he has missed. The girl who felt underprivileged because she was not a boy grows up to be a bossy, aggressive dominating woman whom nobody wants to marry and nobody wants to work for. The adolescents who felt that their parents were repressing them too much take it out on the adult world in general, and become professional rebels; and the adolescents who felt that their parents were too lax seek some leader-figure whose strict commands they delight to obey.

There are so many cases of this kind that, in our more depressed moods, we may well feel that not much progress is really possible without a good deal more understanding of ourselves than we at present possess. But at least we can try to act on this knowledge. We have to be suspicious of those many people, including ourselves, who on paper and in conversation have high ideals and spend a lot of time talking about world problems and politics, but who are unable to relate properly to those closest to them – their wives, their parents, their friends, their brothers and sisters. If a person cannot love those close to him, it is unlikely that he can feel much real or deep affection for humanity in general: and it is thus unlikely that what he supposes himself to be *doing* for humanity in general – the movements he joins, the political ideals he has, the protest marches he goes on – will be of much value. For it is not motivated by love: it is, at least partly, motivated by an unconscious attempt to solve his own problems by using other people.

So the morally educated person will show his PHIL towards those with whom he is in daily contact. This means not only his friends and relations, but also those whom he meets casually and those to whom he stands in some sort of job-relationship – his superiors and inferiors. How does a sixth-former treat a new boy, or the school porter, or the cleaning-women? How does a pretty seventeen-year-old girl treat a nervous and ugly class-mate? These are the sort of tests that might well mark out the morally educated person; better tests, I would guess, than how 'concerned' they say they feel about the underdeveloped countries, or race prejudice, or war.

2. *Fashion is fatal*

In the first chapter of this book (pp. 6–10) we looked at some of the ways in which people tried to escape from the (hard) task of thinking and making up their own minds. One of these was doing what all their friends did, 'conforming to the peer-group'; and a particular aspect of this is what we might call following *fashion*. I'm not thinking here particularly of following fashion in clothes or music – though even in this, 'because everyone else does', or 'because it's modern', seem rather bad reasons for wearing a certain kind of dress or listening to certain kinds of music. I'm thinking more of fashion in behaviour.

But actually, a lot of the behaviour of many people *is* concerned very much with things like clothes and music and cars and various things you can buy easily and quickly. They don't *think* very much at all; they just react with their senses, their eyes and ears, to what is around them; they live in what Plato described as 'the world of sights and sounds'. Only a puritan would think this to be wicked in itself: but of course as a result they don't have much time or incentive to consider how they are behaving towards other people, and this is where it gets dangerous for morality.

Just as there are fashions in dress and pop music, so there are fashions in things like sexual behaviour, manners, and a great many other areas where other people are concerned. For instance, I should guess (and of course I may be wrong) that punctuality – turning up on time – is less in fashion than it was; and certainly introducing one person to another is no longer such a strong convention as it used to be. Even things like not returning someone else's property, or being prepared to live off other people, may have become fashionable.

The morally educated person will choose his own fashion of behaviour, and he will choose it by trying to determine what conventions or other behaviour is in other people's interests. Of course this may vary. If a girl and boy make a date, and neither of them *minds* if the other turns up an hour late or even doesn't bother to come at all, then being late doesn't matter; but if you're dealing with somebody who wants you to be on time (and most people do, in fact) then it does. Similarly some people may not mind not being introduced to strangers, or positively prefer not to be; but others may feel nervous and want to be introduced. None of this must be dictated by fashion.

It's an interesting and important job to work out just what conventions or fashions are good ones; and the trouble is that people are so influenced by what the current fashion is that they don't even start to work this out. For example, dances used to be organized with every girl having a card with a list of the dances on it: men would come and ask her for a particular dance, and she would put his name down on the card if she wanted to say yes. A lot of formal introductions were made, and in general the whole thing was highly conventionalized. Nowadays the reverse is the case. It is an open question which of these fashions is preferable, which means, I suppose, which of them works best for people having a good time, meeting new people, and so forth. The Victorians blindly followed the first, we blindly follow the second.

3. *Metaphysics and mysticism*

Not so many young people nowadays are passionately attached to the old-style or traditional metaphysical beliefs – I'm thinking particularly of the Christian church. But I doubt if they tend to be any less 'metaphysical' or mystical than before; it's just that the tendency comes out in new ways. One obvious candidate is Marxism; other candidates come and go with contemporary fashion – we have seen 'flower power', 'drop-outs' and 'hippies' of various kinds, people who believe in the spiritual merits of taking drugs, and so on. A good many modern novels, which one might call vaguely 'existentialist', cater for and express this tendency.

Some of these metaphysical outlooks may perhaps be a way of expressing or reinforcing the moral components (PHIL, EMP and so forth) which are what the morally educated person really needs to have. But for the most part, they look suspiciously like another of the escape-routes we noticed in Chapter One. They express the desire to solve life's problems at one blow: to get a quick, total 'answer'. It is depressingly obvious that most of them offer the kind of appeal we should expect – the naïve, hero-figure appeal of a revolutionary leader, the escape-into-another-and-better-world appeal of drugs, the down-with-society-abolish-authority appeal of a utopian political theory. *Of course* these are appealing, particularly perhaps to the young, the impatient, the dissatisfied, the underprivileged, the unloved: but which of us would not like, if he could, to solve life's problems in this quick and easy way?

The morally educated person will not sneer at any of these, because he will not sneer at the people who believe in them. He will take them seriously, but perhaps more seriously as symptoms of dissatisfaction than as intellectually coherent and sensible doctrines. He himself will remember to judge by his use of the moral components, and not by anybody else's mystic or meta-physical doctrines, however much they may appeal to his particular emotions or prejudices. Where the components lead him to take a definite stand on some issue, he will not be afraid to take it; but he will also be careful to make sure that it *is* the components, and not his own private desires (perhaps unknown even to himself), that determine his views.

4. *Respectability and resistance*

Most of our sketches so far have stressed defects which are commonly supposed to be characteristic of young people. This one is supposed to be characteristic of older people; personally I doubt whether either generalization is very sound. There is a large class of people, both young and old, whose errors are not those of wildness or yielding to impulse or fashion. Rather they resist the need to think and act rationally, not by thinking and acting wildly, but rather by doing nothing very much at all. They resist the urgency of morals, the desperate need to put themselves and the world to rights, by inaction. They are respectable, because it is easier to be respectable. They may pretend to some sort of concern about moral problems, but it is mostly lip-service – their emotions are not involved, and their reason is only playing a non-serious game when they consider the problems.

Such people are, perhaps, more common among the middle and upper classes: to be found amongst those who come from a moderately secure and comfortable background, and who have found no particular incentive to engage passionately in life. They may be intelligent, but do not apply their intelligence whole-heartedly to morality. They play safe. They don't want trouble. The young men want a steady job, reasonably well-paid, and a house in a nice residential area; the young women like to be nicely-dressed, clean, respected by the neighbours, and want to be regarded as 'sensible'.

The morally educated person does not sneer at this either. There is nothing wrong with being sensible, or even being clean. But it is not enough. Inside such people, perhaps lying fairly deep

down, are in fact the same passions, fears, desires, loves and hates
that are in all of us. If they are admitted to – if their force is felt
– they can be turned to good effect. We need the power that can
only come from such emotions; without that power, we shall at
best be fairly nice people who don't give much trouble to the
police. In such a person, the moral components are (one might
say) only skin-deep. They have some PHIL towards other people,
they use a bit of EMP and GIG, their KRAT is sufficient to keep
them from doing anything really awful. But they are luke-warm.

I could go on to give a great many more sketches of this kind:
but I think the point should be clear enough. It really amounts
to this: you have to have, and to hold a balance between, *passion*
on the one hand and *patience* on the other. Without passion, we
can never make any progress in morality at all, because we shall
have no incentive; and without patience, we shall just strike out
wildly in various directions and do no real good either to ourselves and other people. Of course it is easy for someone just to
say this on paper, and extremely difficult to carry it out in
practice. But then, if you agree with the aims and objectives, you
can try out all sorts of methods which help you personally. And
it's worth remembering that there is a constant temptation to
forget about the aims and objectives, just because the practice of
it is so difficult: so that it's by no means a waste of time to keep
them constantly before one's mind.

Postscript

Morals, Metaphysics and Mental Health

In this book we have been concerned with one particular area, the area of interpersonal morality. What we've said, in effect, is this: that when other people's interests are involved, what a man does ought to be determined by those interests. We went on to describe the abilities and skills a man would have to possess, if he were to be any good at morality in this sense – awareness of feelings (EMP), enough motivation (KRAT), and so forth.

But is this *all* that we could mean by 'morals'? Doesn't morality also have something to do with what people *feel* (not just with how they act or the reasons for their acting), and with what general outlooks they have on life? Isn't it connected in some way with their ideals and their religion (if they have one), and perhaps ultimately with their sanity or mental health? In particular, aren't there some questions which can't be settled by reference to other people's interests, in the way that we settle questions of interpersonal morality? These are difficult questions, and I'm not going to pretend that we can answer them here. What we can do, though, is to sketch the outline of an answer which will at least show us the kind of abilities we need – the way in which we ought to learn to think – in order to settle our worries about our feelings, ideals, religions and so forth.

First, we have to distinguish between two quite different questions:

(1) Aren't there problems about ideals, religion, etc. which we can't settle by reference to other people's interests?

(2) Wouldn't it be right to call these problems 'moral'?

The answer to (1) is certainly 'Yes'. The answer to (2) is uncertain: to answer it properly we'd have first to look at all the different kinds of 'other problems' mentioned in (1), and then see how the word 'moral' was normally used, and then say which of the kinds of problems the normal use of 'moral' fitted. I am not going to try to answer (2), because it seems rather an academic and unimportant question. What matters is to understand the different kinds of problems: if we understand them and their differences, it doesn't matter much whether we *call* them 'moral' or not.

Secondly, there are lots of *different* cases where we might think that something was wrong, but where other people's interests hadn't been offended. For instance, I may be addicted to smoking and end up with constant bronchitis and lung cancer: or I may fall in love with the wrong girl and make an unhappy marriage: or I may be misled by the glamour of some job and take it up, only to find that I'm not happy in it: or I may have unreasonable fears of spiders, or heights, or running water, or the boss. Again, I may have an absurd admiration for Hitler, or worship some ridiculous or cruel god like Baal, or have some ideal about 'honour' which makes me constantly fight duels like gunfighters in Westerns.

There is a whole range of cases here, but they have one important thing in common. If we ask ourselves what is wrong about them, we are likely to think that something has gone wrong with the person's *feelings* or *emotions*. Of course when this happens, it's true that other people's interests are likely to suffer – as for instance if I wrongly admire Hitler and join the Nazis and start killing Jews, or if I fall in love with the wrong girl and make her unhappy in my marriage as well as myself. But something has gone wrong *before* other people suffer: my emotions are misdirected or inappropriate. So I want to lump all these cases together, for our purposes, and take a closer look at some of them – particularly those that we describe under the titles of 'religions' or 'ideals'.

Origins of religions and ideals

As we can see already, it's simply not good enough to say that what sort of religion or ideal a person has is just 'a matter of taste'. Religions or ideals can be *wrong* (misguided, prejudiced, unreasonable, insane). But what kind of wrongness is it? In order to see this we must take a look at the way in which emotions enter into this area.

For human beings, the world does not consist only of scientific or empirical facts. Things in the world are not only red, square, and heavy, but also frightening, admirable, sad and glorious. Growing up, we have to structure both our sense-experience and our emotional experience into some kind of reliable and stable pattern. We invest (one might say) our emotions, more or less permanently, in certain objects. Everybody does this. For various reasons, the world of sense-objects is remarkably similar for nearly all of us: but the world of emotion-objects is often very different. Nevertheless, every sane person inhabits an emotional world which is sufficiently constant for him to feel tolerably at home in it. The furniture of this world may consist of people, physical objects, words, ideas, equations, images, or anything to which he may attach emotions: and there are no logical limits to this. Any sane person, then, may be said to have an emotional 'outlook': and the comparative stability and adequacy of this outlook may be said to 'make sense of life' for him. In other words, his emotional life is (a) sufficiently ordered for him not to feel lost, over-anxious, uncertain or disintegrated, and (b) sufficiently adequate or worth while for him not to feel it to be boring, pointless, or devoid of pleasure.

'Outlook' is a sufficiently general word to include the whole range of very different cases in which we are interested. This range may be imagined as extending from an unsophisticated, theory-free case where a man simply and regularly feels certain emotions in relation to certain objects, to the highly articulated, theory-laden, 'system-building' case where a man casts his emotions into some well-structured form that has every right to be called a metaphysic or a religion. One can move along the range, e.g. from (i) the man who just doesn't like women very much, via (ii) the man who thinks that women are 'irrational', 'inferior' or 'untrustworthy', and (iii) the man who thinks that 'the place of women is in the home' or that 'women are meant to take orders from men', to (iv) the man who holds a full-blown metaphysical or religious theory, according to which God has made woman to take the lower place (combined with mutually supporting arguments and instances from within his metaphysical system).

A set of scientific beliefs is established, defended or attacked by the usual methods of verification and falsification: we talk here of tests, experiments, balancing the evidence, considering the probabilities – and this kind of talk is not at home in considering ideals, metaphysics or religions. Even if metaphysicians or religious believers were to accept it, they would no longer be engaged in metaphysical or religious thinking, but in a kind of science. What characterizes ideals and metaphysics is what characterizes other 'outlooks' (in our sense): namely, emotional investment in certain objects. To have an ideal, or a religious or metaphysical outlook, is already to be committed to certain attitudes and behaviour. The commitment is made because of the emotional needs and the emotional investment which is enshrined in the outlook: and the only point at which criticism can touch the metaphysician is the point at which his emotional needs become apparent. It is impossible to discuss the rationality of views which flow in this way from metaphysical outlooks without considering the rationality of the emotional investment which themselves sustain the metaphysics which enshrine them.

Morals incorporated into ideals

Thus to most Christians, I would guess, the question, 'Why should we do the will of God?' appears logically odd or unreal, and rightly, because the concept of God in Christianity already has a certain emotional investment attached to it. If the investment were not made, we would not be talking about the Christian God but about something else. Here again criticism must be directed at the first steps: that is, at the original building up of certain emotions and attitudes – at the belief that a certain kind of God is worth worshipping. It is not so much that religious believers really want to *derive* their morality *from* their religion. A better description of how they actually think might be to say that their ideals *take the form of* religious beliefs.

There are, of course, senses in which an ideal or metaphysical outlook offers a man *some* kind of reason, when he is defending *particular* moral beliefs or actions. If a man believes (say) in some metaphysical ideal which might be expressed by him as 'the spirit of the German nation' or 'Arab destiny', then he may defend his action (a) as realizing that ideal in a particular instance, or (b) as promoting some state of affairs which would realize that ideal. Thus (a) if part of what he means by 'Arab destiny' is conquering Israel, then if he joins an Israel-conquering army he is therein fulfilling Arab destiny; (b) if he stays in Egypt and knits socks for the soldiers, he may prefer to say that, though he is not himself fulfilling Arab destiny, he is making it possible for Arab destiny to be fulfilled. Again, a man who believes in the ideal of a sexually chaste society may object to pornographic literature because (a) a society which sells such literature would not count for him as a sexually chaste society – the existence of such literature would count directly against his ideal; or (b) because, though he does not mind such literature in itself, he thinks that it will incite people to sexual licence, which latter would of course count directly against his ideal.

But what this shows is, again, the importance of obtaining criteria for the original ideal or emotional investment. For the kind of reasons in the example above are (we would want to say) only reasons for *that* man: why should *we* feel like this about Arab destiny or a chaste society? Or, again, even if we grant that one ideal or metaphysic may be right or reasonable for one man, and another for another, must we not also say that (at least in some cases) an ideal or metaphysic may be wrong or unreasonable for any man, or that it may be wrong or unreasonable for the particular man who adopts it? Surely we must say this. To take a parallel, the fact that different drugs suit different medical cases is perfectly consistent, as we very well know, with the facts (a) that some drugs may be harmful for everyone, (b) that a particular drug may be harmful for a particular person. In other words, there will be criteria to be applied for ideals and metaphysics, as for drugs, in each case, even though it may be true that we ought not all to have the same drugs or the same ideals and metaphysics.

How then are we to handle this class of cases, where what is in question is a man's 'outlook' – his ideals, or metaphysical views, or religious beliefs? I am suggesting that this class of cases is essentially similar to the class of cases which we normally deal with under the title of 'mental health', and that the kinds of unreason here are like the kinds of unreason that we find in those who are, to a greater or lesser degree, mentally ill. In particular, it is lack of rationality in the sphere of a man's *emotions* that seems particularly relevant.

The Moral Components again
If we now try to face the general question, 'How do we tell whether or not we are being unreasonable in cases concerned with "mental health", ideals, and religious or other "outlooks"?', there are various kinds of answers we can give. Often people have given one sort of answer, which seems mistaken. They have assumed that we *already know* which ideals, religious beliefs, etc. are right and sensible. The mistake here is like the mistake we noticed earlier[1] about morals: that of supposing that we can decide straightaway what is morally right and wrong. But of course we can't decide this without first knowing *how* to decide.

[1] pp. 28–29.

Apart from this mistaken answer, people have for the most part only talked in a very general way about the qualities which you need to deal with these cases. It is easy enough to say that, when trying to choose between different ideals, you need 'imagination', 'experience', 'wisdom', 'understanding' and so on; or that mentally healthy people are 'integrated', 'balanced', 'mature', etc.; or that to avoid imprudence you must be 'sensible', 'far-sighted', 'responsible', or whatever. It is also fairly easy to sketch out the ways in which one might try to help a person deal with such cases. For instance, one might describe different kinds of ideals to him, or show him how various religions worked out in practice; or one might try to help him to be prudent by showing him the consequences of various courses of action. But all this seems rather too vague and general to be of much help. We need to know what *kinds of mistakes* can be made, and what kinds of skills and abilities are needed.

The short answer to this is fairly simple: we need those skills and abilities which we have already listed in reference to morality – first in general terms (pp. 44–47), and then by describing our 'moral components' (pp. 50–66). A fuller answer would involve a good deal more work than we have space for; but it is possible to make one or two useful points:

1. Of the components, PHIL (caring for other people, regarding them as equals, etc.) and DIK (a mode of reasoning based on other people's interests), are not here relevant, for we are here dealing with cases where other people's interests do not come into the matter. Similarly GIG (2) ('social skills') is irrelevant. On the other hand, the other components are plainly very relevant: i.e. GIG (1) (knowledge of 'hard' facts), EMP (awareness of one's own and other people's feelings), and KRAT (motivation for bringing GIG and EMP to bear, and for acting and feeling accordingly).

2. Because of the importance of the rationality of a person's emotions to his ideals and outlooks, GIG (1) is likely to be of less significance than the other two relevant components (EMP and KRAT). When people are mentally ill, or have unreasonable out-

looks on life, the basic difficulty is not usually that they do not
know enough hard facts. It is rather that they are not aware of
their own feelings and the feelings of other people (EMP), or that
they lack the self-control, motivation, etc. to allow this awareness
to operate effectively. There are of course simple cases where false
beliefs lead to mistaken or unreasonable outlooks. For example,
if I genuinely believe that all Jews are plotting to overthrow the
state, or that all Negroes behave like animals, then somebody
could show me that these beliefs were false, and I would change
my attitude. This would not be a case of *prejudice*, but just a
case of ignorance. But there are very many cases where what
happens is not so simple: where there is some hidden reason why
I hate Jews or despise Negroes, why I am infatuated with a
worthless girl, why I am unduly scared of my boss, unreasonably anxious to impress my friends with my strength or
importance, irrationally disposed to believe that people hate
me, unable to face life without relying on a god or a leader-
figure to stand over me, and so on. It is example of this kind
which make the cases which we are concerned with so difficult in
practice.

3. Much of the difficulty arises because it rarely happens that
human beings quite straightforwardly want this, or decide to do
that, or believe the other. They are very often in a state of conflict. Not all their emotions and beliefs are on the surface, in their
conscious minds: it often happens that they have a set of *unconscious* emotions and beliefs which work against their conscious
ones. They may not admit these emotions and beliefs to themselves, or only in moments of extreme honesty and self-awareness
– moments which often pass all too quickly. It is not only possible,
but very common, for a person to deny, even to himself, that he
feels frightened, or small, or insecure, or impotent: and to pretend
to himself and to others that he is confident, powerful and brave.
And so in many other cases.

It is this which often accounts for a lack of proper motivation,
resolution, and sincerity (KRAT), and which makes the practical
application of self-awareness and the awareness of others (EMP)

so complicated. A person's general outlook on life, which will include his prudence or imprudence, his ideals and his religion or lack of religion, is a product of his total personality: his childhood fears and desires, his later experiences, the beliefs and emotions that he once felt but has now perhaps forgotten and repressed (yet which continue to influence him). To unravel all of these, to make him properly aware of what he feels, to free him from those compulsions and false beliefs which prevent him from behaving reasonably, is obviously an endless task. But there is no other way.

Further Reading

First, have another look at what we said in Chapter One (p. 15) about the use of books. It's not much good reading a great deal if it doesn't help you to think: it's essential that you should clearly understand what you read: and it's highly desirable that you should discuss it and argue about it with other people.

Next, you ought to know that there are a great many very bad books on morality. Reading some of them may be not only a waste of time, but positively dangerous: for some of them do no more than try to persuade you to share the author's prejudices, or sell you some particular 'philosophy' or way of life. What they try to sell may be very attractive to you, because it may happen to fit your own prejudices: but you should be aware all the more. The questions to ask yourself about any book are:

   (i) Is it clearly written, not confused or 'waffle'?
  (ii) Is it workmanlike, sensible and reasonable?
 (iii) Does it actually help you to *think*, or help to solve any problems?

Next, you will have gathered from Chapter One (p. 14) that questions about morality will come under one or other of the relevant disciplines – usually philosophy, psychology or sociology. There are experts in these subjects, and if you are not sure who the experts are you can consult your teachers (who ought to know), or else find out from a professor or lecturer at some reputable university. The suggested books that follow will give you some help in this respect.

Introduction to Moral Education, by John Wilson and others (Penguin). The easiest thing to do is to get hold of this book, read it, and then use the book-list at the back of it, which contains suggestions for further reading in the philosophy, psychology and sociology of morals. But the following may be particularly useful:

Contemporary Moral Philosophy, G. J. Warnock (Macmillan);
Thinking with Concepts, John Wilson (C.U.P.);
Freedom and Reason, R. M. Hare (O.U.P.);
A Short History of Ethics, A. C. MacIntyre (Macmillan);
Man, Morals and Society, J. C. Flugel (Penguin);
The Challenge of Youth, (ed.) Erik Erikson (Doubleday);
The Assessment of Morality, John Wilson (N.F.E.R. Publications);
Sociology, Barry Sugarman (Heinemann);
Education and the Concept of Mental Health, John Wilson (Routledge);
Education, Alan Harris (Heinemann).

Morality is a vast topic, and there are lots of other books worth reading. But after you've read one or two of these and discussed them, you'll have a better idea of what aspects of the topic you're interested in. Then you can easily take advice about what other books you'll want to read. Above all, don't give up or get lost. Some people never read anything about this at all, and other people get bogged down in a lot of very long and muddled books which they don't find helpful. You'll do best if you keep the questions you're interested in clearly in mind, and use whatever books help you to answer them.